W9-BKZ-809

# Hurricane
# Hugo
## and the
# Grand Strand

# Hurricane Hugo and the Grand Strand

The majority of the contents of this book is
by Sun News staffers and appeared in The Sun News
as part of its coverage of Hurricane Hugo,
Sept. 21-Oct. 15, 1989.

Edited by Cynthia J. Struby

# Foreword

As you move along the coast, from the Brunswick County, N.C., beaches to Little River, North Myrtle Beach, Atlantic Beach, Briarcliffe Acres, Myrtle Beach, Surfside Beach, Garden City, Murrells Inlet, Pawleys Island and Georgetown, you see the lives and livelihoods of residents and businesses crunched and splintered.

You can sense the hurt and suffering of the people since Hurricane Hugo's visit to the Myrtle Beach Area. The pain in the pit of your stomach and the taste of bile in your throat won't go away.

You want to cry, but you can't. There's no time. There's no time because it's time to rebuild and renew.

You see it in the eyes of your neighbor. Behind the pain and the tears runs a stubborn streak that screams, "You can give me your best shot, Hugo, but you can't put me down for the count."

The Myrtle Beach Area cleanup moves ahead swiftly. The people of the Myrtle Beach Area simply refuse to give in or give up.

This book is dedicated to those people.

They are our friends and neighbors. They love living at the beach. The sand in their shoes is permanent, and so are they.

We are proud to be a part of this community, proud to be a part of this strong-willed populace who, through Hugo, have learned to live together better, to love each other a little more and to never give up.

Special thanks go to the employees of The Sun News. Each made significant contributions to our coverage of Hurricane Hugo. We dedicated massive resources to make sure that our coverage area knew everything we did. From the time Hugo started to peek at the Myrtle Beach Area, through the completion of our Hurricane Hugo Special Edition, and continuing through the cleanup and renewal of our home town, we have made every effort to give you a complete, interesting, timely, compelling newspaper. We hope you are pleased.

Some of the proceeds from this book will go to the Myrtle Beach Area Hugo Economic Renewal Fund and The Sun News Educational Foundation.

We hope this book will help you see the magnitude of the effort needed to rebuild and renew our home town. We also hope you will see the spirit of our people.

We're coming back on fast-forward.

*J. Michael Pate*

J. Michael Pate
Publisher and President
The Sun News

# The Life Of Hurricane Hugo

**Saturday, Sept. 9, 1989:**
A group of thunderstorms leaves the coast of Africa near Dakar.

**Sunday, Sept. 10:**
The storm is upgraded to a tropical depression as it moves over the Cape Verde Islands, west of Africa. A tropical depression has winds of up to 38 miles per hour.

**Monday, Sept. 11:**
The tropical depression continues to move westward and is upgraded again, to Tropical Storm Hugo. Tropical storms are named and have wind of 39 to 73 miles per hour.

**Tuesday, Sept. 12:**
Tropical Storm Hugo continues its westward path across the Atlantic Ocean.

**Wednesday, Sept. 13:**
Hugo's wind speed increases, and it is upgraded to hurricane status. A Category 1 hurricane has winds of 74 to 95 miles per hour; Category 2 has winds of 96 to 110 miles per hour; Category 3 has wind speeds of 111 to 130 miles per hour.

**Thursday, Sept. 14:**
Hugo continues to pick up wind speed and moves westward, toward the Caribbean.

**Friday, Sept. 15:**
Hurricane Hugo's winds are 150 miles per hour, a Category 4 hurricane (wind speeds of 131 to 155 miles per hour). It is about 400 miles east-southeast of Guadeloupe, moving westward at 15 miles per hour.

**Saturday, Sept. 16:**
Hugo is moving west-northwest at 12 miles per hour, with winds of 140 miles per hour. It is just east of Guadeloupe and the other Leeward Islands.

**Sunday, Sept. 17:**
Hugo hits Guadeloupe and other Leeward Islands with 140 mile-per-hour winds. About two dozen people are killed and about 27,500 left homeless on the islands. There is heavy damage to property, and communication systems and utilities are disrupted.

**Monday, Sept. 18:**
Eastern Puerto Rico and the U.S. Virgin Islands are pounded by Hugo's 125-mile-per-hour winds. At least 18 are dead. Puerto Rico reports an estimated $1.1 billion in damages, including crop losses and lost industrial production. Homes of 50,000 are destroyed or damaged. In St. Croix, about 90% of the homes are damaged or destroyed, leaving most of the island's 55,000 people at least temporarily homeless. Extensive damage to businesses from widespread looting is reported, including raids by ma-chete-wielding gangs. Expending much of its energy over the islands, Hugo is downgraded to Category 2 status.

**Tuesday, Sept. 19:**
Hugo takes a swipe at the Bahamas with 105 mile-per-hour winds and moves northeast of Grand Turk Island, a British island off the south Bahamas. The hurricane continues its path northwestward at 12 miles per hour.

**Wednesday, Sept. 20:**
Hugo rebuilds in strength and hurricane watches are issued for St. Augustine, Fla., to Cape Hatteras, N.C. "Watch" status means a hurricane could occur within 36 hours.

**Thursday, Sept. 21:**
Hurricane Hugo is predicted to hit the U.S. coast somewhere north of Charleston, S.C. Gov. Carroll Campbell orders a mandatory evacuation of all S.C. beach areas as Hugo is upgraded again to Category 4.

**Friday, Sept. 22:**
Hugo slams into the S.C. coast around midnight with 135 mile-per-hour winds. At least 18 are killed in South Carolina. Some 64,000 are left homeless, and 270,000 are left jobless.

The state Department of Insurance estimates $3.17 billion in insured losses alone, but many homes are uninsured. Agricultural losses are estimated at $67 million, including timber. Gov. Campbell says damage in the state is $4 billion to $5 billion.

The storm destroys about 5,400 S.C. homes, according to the American Red Cross.

Almost 18,000 miles of roads in the state are damaged or covered with debris, according to highway department officials.

About 5,900 structures in North Myrtle Beach, Myrtle Beach, Georgetown County and Charleston are damaged or destroyed, says a S.C. Coastal Council spokeswoman. Electricity, water and sewer services are knocked out.

National Guardsmen are brought in to hard-hit areas to prevent looting, enforce curfews and prevent sightseeing.

Fierce winds whip Charlotte, N.C., overturning and snapping trees. Damage is estimated at more than $370 million.

Twenty-two S.C. counties and 13 N.C. counties will be declared disaster areas.

By mid-Friday, Hugo is downgraded to a tropical storm and loses even that designation when its winds drop below 40 miles per hour around Pittsburgh.

**Saturday, Sept. 23:**
The storm causes one death in New York when a tree limb falls on a car, killing a passenger. Hugo's remnants then are absorbed by a stronger weather front in eastern Canada.

Compiled from Sun News staff and wire reports

# Hurricane Hugo and the Grand Strand

**Editor:**
Cynthia J. Struby

**Assistants:**
Sue Deans
Linda E. Jensen
Beth Terry

**Mechanicals:**
Christine H. Hunt

**Pre-press camera work:**
Clyde Owens
Bennie Stephens

**Photographers:**
Catherine P. Black
Chris Germann
Bill Heath
Barbara N. Heyward
Wendy Hilts
Cecelia Konyn
Bryan Monroe
Steve Schaefer
Bill Scroggins
Charles Slate
Cynthia J. Struby

**Reporters:**
Leon Barrineau
Mel Derrick
Chrysti Edge
Sammy Fretwell
Chris Germann
Lisa Greene
David Hill
Melissa Huff
Rebecca James
Yolanda Jones
Cecelia Konyn
Bob Kudelka
Caroline McDonald
Bryan Monroe
Ron Morrison
Ettie Newlands
Mona Prufer
Joseph J. Serwach
Andrew Shain
Lesia J. Shannon
Gil Thelen
Danny Young

# Contents

# 'I've never seen anything like it . . .

**By David Hill**
THE SUN NEWS

Will Prioleau drove down to Pawleys Island from Columbia Saturday morning to see what Hurricane Hugo had done to his beach house. When he got there he climbed to the top of the roof.

It wasn't a hard climb.

The top of the roof was only 6 feet above the ground.

The storm surge, probably 14 feet deep, had sawed the house and roof apart. The part Prioleau stood on came to rest across the street from the foundation.

Four or five houses were crammed into one big mass of lumber, shingles and siding.

Porcelain toilets were filled with sand.

An upright vacuum cleaner lay in one pile of rubble.

A car engine lay where a house once stood; apparently, someone had been overhauling it.

An unopened can of Budweiser beer rested in the sand nearby, but there was no telling if it had come from Prioleau's house.

In the distance, rugged wooden planks stuck up six feet out of the beach.

Two days earlier, all but the top 10 inches or so had been buried in fine, white beach sand. The planks had been a seawall. Someone actually thought they could hold back the ocean.

Instead, the ocean came and took whatever it wanted. People who grew up in coastal South Carolina always knew it would.

Hurricanes, we were told as each season began on June 1, are as much a fact of beach life as surf and tides.

We knew that, even though storm after storm — David, Diana, Gloria, Bob, Kate — brushed South Carolina without ever really striking. We knew a major hurricane was inevitable, even though we might have allowed ourselves to think otherwise.

Maybe some unknown freakish change in sea or air currents had

come to protect us.

Maybe the Gulf Stream had shifted just enough to divert hurricanes away from the little indentation on the continent where the state lies.

Maybe hurricanes would keep striking the Gulf Coast, Florida — but never *here*.

Then sometime around midnight on Thursday, Sept. 21-Friday, Sept. 22, Hurricane Hugo, the eighth named storm of the 1989 North Atlantic hurricane season, struck. Hugo shattered any illusions that we might have had.

The inevitable had happened. And we were living it, from the evacuations the morning before to a week later, when the storm was nothing but a mass of clouds indistinguishable from a cold front it had joined in Canada, to a month after, when debris still littered the oceanfront and living trees were still brown with windblown leaves and dead ones still lay on the ground.

"I think the hardest thing for people to understand if they haven't seen it is, even if you have a home to go back to, everything is covered with mud," said Debbie Thames, whose McClellanville hardware store was flooded nearly 6 feet deep — though it's more than a quarter-mile from the nearest body of water.

"They sent us barbecue grills, and that seems like a very nice gesture. But there's no food to cook, there are no back yards to cook in.

"I'm not saying this just to say, 'Oh, poor us.' It's that bad here."

**Natural disasters** were no longer something that happened in the Caribbean islands or Mexico — something played out on television or in newspapers. Instead, a 70-foot-tall pine laid itself in your kitchen. A fishing boat came to rest in the street outside. You or someone you know was homeless and had lost all possessions that couldn't be carried out in the car. You couldn't illuminate your kitchen, cook your food or keep it from spoiling. You'd spent the night in a high school gymnasium, and now that you were home,

troops in camouflage fatigues and carrying automatic rifles patrolled the entrance to your neighborhood, and you couldn't go out after dark.

People were killed by a hurricane — right here in South Carolina.

Nature was no longer a beautiful, benign thing; it was now a vicious, destructive force.

Page Oberlin, owner of the Sea View Inn on Pawleys Island, walked the beach to see the damage first-hand one afternoon. She noticed a flock of birds flying overhead that, looking down, abandoned their "V" formation. They seemed confounded by what they saw. It just wasn't right any more.

For her own part, Oberlin said, the destruction was worse than she could ever imagine.

"I don't have that kind of imagination," she said.

"I've never seen anything like it," said National Guard Sgt. Dennis Nesbit, who lives in Georgetown and guarded the entrance to Litchfield Beach. "I hope I never do again. Let's hope it stays away for another 50 decades."

**For many people** who live on the coast, Hurricane Hugo will become the new benchmark by which future storms are judged.

Until Hugo — and even as it approached — people kept referring to two storms, Gracie in September 1959, which struck Beaufort and Charleston hard, and Hazel, an October 1954 storm that is legendary on the Grand Strand.

Hazel wiped out much of then-fledgling Myrtle Beach, and it's the storm to which all others since have been compared.

To many people, Hazel was used as the historical reference point much the way World War II is: A town of small family-owned cottages became a major, high-rise resort as landowners sold out out to large developers.

Eddie Carraway was in his late 20s in 1954 and had joined Georgetown County's Red Cross a year earlier. He was one of the first back to

10

# ...I hope I never do again'

Pawleys Island after Hazel struck. Now county Civil Defense director, Carraway still has a Hazel tracking map on his office wall and photos of the island afterward.

On the Thursday night when Hugo churned toward Charleston, Carraway brought out some black-and-white photos of Pawleys Island after Hazel. They were passed around among some of the 30 or so people gathered in the boarded-up Civil Defense office.

He talked about how the only information about hurricanes in those days came from ship reports, and how the city police station was then in the Rice Museum. Today's technology made hurricane tracking more precise, but it still couldn't keep the storms away.

When a mid-evening status report came from the National Hurricane Center that showed Hugo had strengthened and was headed for some unknown point between Charleston and the North Carolina line, Carraway took a breather and sat down in his office chair.

"My God, I never thought I'd live to see the day," he said. "We've got another Hazel."

If there had been any doubt a serious storm was on the way, it was now gone.

**When we awoke** Friday morning — if we'd gone to sleep at all — beaches we knew were not the same.

Where Hazel's eye had passed the northern Grand Strand called Cherry Grove, Hugo had again tossed beach houses off the oceanfront. Beach sand was gouged out several feet deep.

Elsewhere, many hotels and condominiums had lost oceanfront pools and decks. Some had lost their entire first floors.

Every fishing pier between Folly Beach and North Carolina was destroyed. Chunks of some were still standing, and pilings a couple hundred feet offshore stuck up out of the surf where others had stood. But in most cases, there was hardly a sign

any pier ever existed.

As Friday afternoon arrived, it became clear that some of the worst damage was to the south. Surfside Beach had been hit hard. Houses bounced across Ocean Boulevard into the second row. A woman in Long Bay Estates said, "I can't find my house."

Stretches of Garden City, particularly on the narrow sandy peninsula that extends seaward of Murrells Inlet, were wiped clean. The Kingfisher Pier was obliterated. Condominiums rising a dozen stories over the beach still stood, surprising more than a few people.

We'd always heard it said that these high-rises up and down the beach would "fall into the ocean," and we had conjured up images of these giant buildings toppling to the beach. As we returned that Friday, we wondered with a mix of fascination and fear if we would see that both awful and fantastic sight.

It didn't happen; the high-rises still stood. But somehow the sight of the cracked pools and the cut-away motels seemed worse than that imagined picture. This, after all, was no longer just imagination. It was real.

Individual homes had suffered most. Lynn Kirtley found his new home all alone on the oceanfront in the block south of the Kingfisher in Garden City. Six houses had stood between the high-rise and the house. "I hope insurance declares it totaled," Kirtley said. "I know that's awful to say, but it's twisted and the stairs are gone. I mean, look, there's nothing to come back here for."

**In Murrells Inlet,** seagoing fishing boats large enough to be homes at sea for days at a time, were tossed on shore next to seafood restaurants. Some of the eateries, which contributed to the inlet's claim as the "Seafood Capital of South Carolina," were no longer whole.

Pawleys Island, one of the nation's first summer beach resorts, was as hard-hit as Garden City. One of the apparent losses was a cottage

called the Summer Academy, bought two years ago for more than $900,000. It had gotten its name from housing a boys' summer school in the 19th century. It had survived Hazel, even the storm of 1893, in which houses were taken to sea with oil lamps burning and faces pressed against windows. Sea water covered the Waccamaw Neck. But this time, the Summer Academy would not be spared.

**Just days after Hugo left,** people were helping each other. There were looters and price gougers — $10 for a 79-cent bag of ice, for example — but people who had lost their homes were thankful they had friends to stay with and were not alone. Donations flooded aid agencies. Restaurants gave away free meals. People who suffered losses themselves hurried to clean up so they could help others.

R.D. Berry of McClellanville had his house flooded during the storm but was just as concerned with getting his general store in operation for his stricken customers.

"Elderly people came up to the store," he said, "and the food they bought the day before was fine, but their house was gone. I've got to get my store opened."

Mark Garner, a former Myrtle Beach mayor who lived through Hurricane Hazel, recalled how the area pulled together and rebuilt, making 1954 a benchmark in Grand Strand history. Hugo may be the same, Garner said, suggesting that years from now those who live here may look back on September 1989 as a new starting point.

"It's gonna change some things," said Alan Altman, a real estate broker who grew up on Pawleys Island. "But there's enough left to create a foothold where we can pull ourselves back up.

"Maybe Mother Nature will be nice. Another 35 years would be nice."

Edited by Cindy Burton and Lineta Pritchard

**This motorist had the right idea while evacuating Myrtle Beach on Thursday afternoon.** Photographer: Bryan Monroe

**Residents line up Wednesday for free water at Surfside Beach City Hall.** Photographer: Chris Germann

**"I cannot believe when you have an emergency order in effect that a state elected official would (do that),"** said S.C. Gov. Carroll Campbell, about a state legislator who went surfing during a mandatory evacuation order. Reporter: Chrysti Edge

**Surfers try to get in some last-minute waves in Garden City Thursday morning before Hurricane Hugo hit.** Photographer: Charles Slate

**Phillip Greene tapes up a window of the Beachcomber Motel Wednesday afternoon as residents prepared for Hurricane Hugo.**
Photographer: Steve Schaefer

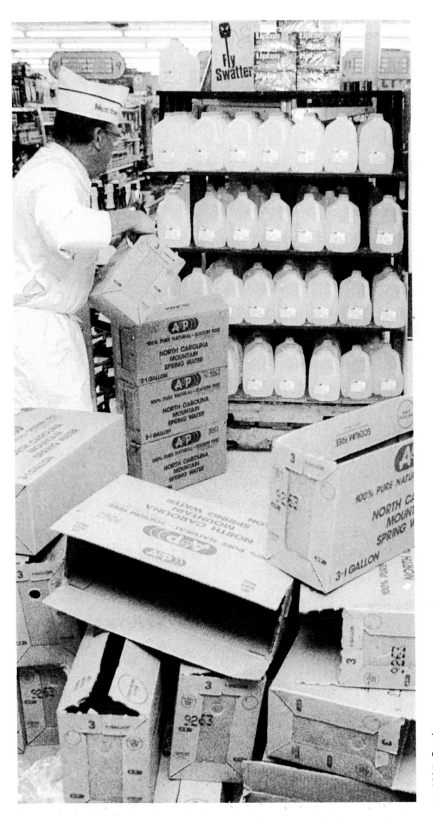

"You've heard the old adage: When the wind holds the plyboard against the window, then you start nailing the plyboard. I plan right now to be open tomorrow night," said David Brittain of the Sea Captain's House and the Caribbean Motel on Sept. 20.

Reporter: Lesia J. Shannon

**Tommy Martin stocks the shelves of the A&P on 29th Avenue North in Myrtle Beach with jugs of water the day before Hugo hit the South Carolina coast.** Photographer: Bill Scroggins

The halls of Myrtle Beach High School began to fill up the day before Hugo hit, as weather reports brought the hurricane closer to Myrtle Beach. Later Thursday, those at the high school shelter were evacuated 14 miles inland to Conway. Photographer: Steve Schaefer

Ansonio Carter, 14 months, eats his dinner with the help of dad, Randy, while mom, Angela, looks on Thursday night in the Conway High School evacuation shelter. Photographer: Chris Germann

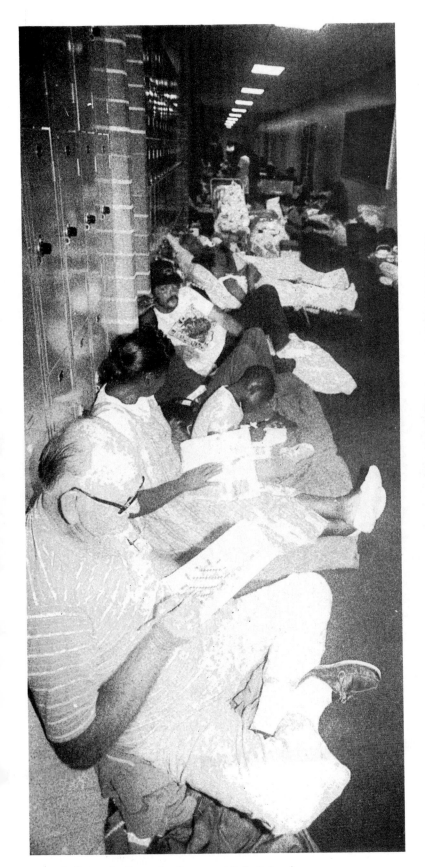

Monique and her brother, John Sumter, were at the Myrtle Beach High School evacuation site, waiting for Hugo to pass. As the hurricane approached Myrtle Beach, they were evacuated to another shelter in Conway. Photographer: Steve Schaefer

"We can't make them leave, but if they refuse to leave, we'll get their names and addresses and next of kin," said Georgetown Police officer Michael Poole when area evacuation was ordered Sept. 21. Reporter: Rebecca James

**People line a hallway in Conway High School Thursday night, doing crosswords and reading to pass the time. More than 3,000 people took shelter at the high school.** Photographer: Chris Germann

**"Everybody's nice until they want to go to their homes," said S.C. National Guard Pfc. Randall McLain of Cheraw.** Reporter: Lesia J. Shannon

**Patrol cars on Friday block the entrance into North Myrtle Beach via the old U.S. 17 bridge.** Photographer: Chris Germann

Traffic backs up on the Intracoastal Waterway bridge into North Myrtle Beach as homeowners try to return to their homes on **Friday.** Photographer: Charles Slate

"The problem with everyone is losing your temper — on our side and on the public's side," said Charles Sendler, North Myrtle Beach Police Chief. "Sometimes when people can't get in, they take it out on us, and sometimes our officers take it out on them."
Reporter: Melissa Huff

S.C. State Patrol officers check IDs before letting residents return to Myrtle Beach on **Friday.** Photographer: Chris Germann

**"The Lord helped us get this, and the Lord will help us get more,"** said Richard Brown, **McClellanville resident.** Reporter: Melissa Huff

McClellanville shrimping boats were carried ashore and parked next to this large home. The storm surge left watermarks 6 feet up on buildings a quarter-mile from the marsh.
Photographer: Bill Scroggins

"When I lay down on the pillow, the tears just flow. I have nightmares. Like I'm fighting for my life again," said Mary Linen. "But I still say we are blessed. . . . Everyone wants to come back. If we didn't, we'd pass by all this." Reporter: Melissa Huff

Mary Linen and her brother-in-law, Larry Linen, talk about their experience surviving the hurricane. Photographer: Chris Germann

**Ashley Phillips of Knoxville, Tenn., plays on a pile of rubble caused by Hurricane Hugo near the boat landing in McClellanville. Ashley was in town with his family to help his grandmother, aunt and uncle clean up their house, which was damaged by the hurricane.** Photographer: Chris Germann

A McClellanville home, severely damaged by Hugo. The town is about a mile inland, shielded from the ocean by Cape Romain, a wide marsh, and the Intracoastal Waterway. Photographer: Chris Germann

A pelican, apparently killed by the winds and flooding of Hurricane Hugo, lies in the debris near the boat landing in McClellanville. Photographer: Chris Germann

Shrimp boats, like the Patricia Anne, were bounced around the waterfront. An unidentified couple walks among the ruins.
Photographer: Chris Germann

"I don't know if I can ever listen to wind again and not get scared," said Debbie Thames of McClellanville.
Reporter: David Hill

"I've been through a lot of hurricanes in my life," said R.D. "Buster" Brown, who spent Thursday night on the second floor of his McClellanville home. "I'm from Sullivans Island, and I've never left for a hurricane. It's the worst scare I've seen in my life. I will never, ever, ever ride out a hurricane again." Reporter: David Hill

Marines get a breakfast of scrambled eggs, bacon, grits and hot coffee during the cleanup effort in McClellanville.
Photographer: Bill Scroggins

Hugo's storm surge swept Mary Linen and her two children out of their McClellanville home and onto the porch. Linen grabbed the two children, Lisa Marie, 12, and Christopher, 7, as the porch began to tilt, pushed by the water funneled through narrow Jeremy Creek. The porch stopped moving when it hit a tree and Linen then tied her two children to that tree with an extension cord to keep them from being swept away into the darkness. There, the three rode out the storm. Linen said she still doesn't know how long they were there, but they didn't untie themselves until daybreak. "Lisa put Christopher in a bag and punched a hole in it so he could breathe." Reporter: David Hill

"The Lord is nigh unto them that are of a broken heart."
—Psalm 34:18a

**This printed Bible verse, stamped on a scrap of paper, was found on the floor of a devastated McClellanville home.** Photographer: Bill Scroggins

**Trucks were tossed into and around the McClellanville boat landing.** Photographer: Chris Germann

**This sailboat floated across the Harbourwalk
and ended up high and dry behind the Rice
Museum in downtown Georgetown.**
Photographer: Charles Slate

**Georgetown Landing Marina was severely damaged.** Photographer: Charles Slate

**Docks and buildings along the Riverfront were damaged by high water.** Photographer: Charles Slate

**Boats from the Georgetown Landing Marina were washed ashore and jammed under the U.S. 17 bridge by the storm surge of Hurricane Hugo.** Photographer: Steve Schaefer

As 1989 began, Jerry Merritt decided to move his household from Gainesville, Ga., to the edge of Georgetown's Winyah Bay. He had found his dream house: a two-story Colonial with 10-foot ceilings, windows facing the water and strong columns to support the roof. In early September, he put the finishing touches on the original hardwood floors in the house off Highmarket Street. Now he'll be starting over. A surge from Hurricane Hugo demolished the brick wall that guarded his front yard. The water then burst through the front door and windows and knocked out a window on the side of the house. Water lines were midway up the 10-foot walls and a mud/seaweed mixture was clinging to the ceilings. "I've only been here six months," he said as he looked at his belongings scattered over the muddy lawn. "I don't even have insurance yet." Reporters: Leon Barrineau, Danny Young

Harold Glasgo, 4, discards the cardboard centers from bolts of damaged cloth outside Scott's Stitch & Sew shop on Front Street. Some businesses on Front Street suffered heavy water damage as the Sampit River rose 8½ feet above normal. Photographer: Charles Slate

**Shoes were lined up on the steps drying at this waterfront business.** Photographer: Charles Slate

At Debordieu, the residential and resort development between Pawleys Island and Georgetown, many oceanfront buildings were damaged by the storm surge. Dunes between the homes were obliterated, leaving houses such as this one exposed. Here, water ate away sand around the house's foundation and wave entered beneath the front living room, taking the floor with them. Photographer: David Hill

"The main thing I got was all the houses on pilings made it through. The houses on slabs, it went right through. You shouldn't have a house on the ocean without pilings," said Joe Maloney of Fayetteville, N.C., whose DeBordieu home is away from the ocean. Reporter: David Hill

DeBordieu Colony's golf course was hit especially hard by Hugo. The course suffered the loss of trees and salt water damage. Shown here are the driving range and first hole. The clubhouse, undamaged, is in the upper right. Photographer: Monty Cook.

**This home in the private Debordieu community was destroyed by the hurricane's storm surge.** Photographer: Steve Schaefer

**These sandbags did little to protect the Pawleys Island home that used to stand behind them.** Photographer: Steve Schaefer

Pvt. Anthony Dallas of the HQ 4th/178th Field Artillery unit of the S.C. National Guard in Georgetown County keeps watch on the south end of Pawleys Island, near a storm channel the cut the island in two. The channel was filled five days after Hugo's visit, but high tides washed it out the next day. Photographer: Bill Scroggins

Bob and Derrick Oliver clean out their Pawleys Island home. About 80 of the 300 houses were destroyed. Photographer: Bryan Monroe

**Pawleys Island**

**The Tip Top Inn toppled toward the ocean when its supports were ripped out.** Photographer: Bill Scroggins

**Aerial view along Pawleys Island. The Tip Top Inn tips toward the ocean.** Photographer: Bill Scroggins

**Pawleys Island residents scavenge through the rubble that used to be their homes to find what was left of their belongings.**
Photographer: Steve Schaefer

**Will Prioleau stands on the roof of what was his beachfront home. Hugo moved the house to the third row, destroying it completely. At least three homes were blown across the creek that separates the island from the mainland.** Photographer: Charles Slate

"I walked past it — all the points of reference have changed," said Stokes Smith Jr. of his family's vacation home on the south end of Pawleys Island. "Then I said, 'I know that house and that one — that's where it is.' " But the house was gone. "I found a bunch of stuff from the kitchen on the other side of the creek, but I can't find the house." Reporter: Rebecca James

The motor of a ceiling fan lies on the ground in the approximate spot where the house with its room intact stood before the storm. Homes that had been oceanfront, second row and third row came to rest — if they weren't demolished — among fourth-row houses, or where the fourth row once was. Photographer: David Hill

Barry Klopfer and Robin Thomas console each other after seeing the devastation of Pawleys Island. At least 50 homes — about 1 in every 5 — were destroyed on the island. Photographer: Bryan Monroe

Hurricane Hugo cut a 20-foot storm channel through Pawleys Island, severing its southern section. That southern end of the island, which had virtually no dune protection, had many houses washed away by a 12-feet-high storm surge. Much of the 2-mile-long island is only wide enough for one row of houses, with the ocean on one side and the creek and street on the other.
Photographer: Bill Scroggins

"That's Mary's house," Emily Sawyer said of her Pawleys Island neighbor's home. "Oh, Lord, it's gone. . . . This is the second time in my life I've been through the same thing. I lost a house in Hazel; can you believe I built another one?" Reporter: Rebecca James

**Chairs and pictures were tossed about and glass was broken inside Pawleys Island Chapel.** Photogragher: Bill Scroggins

A Pawleys Island woman makes her way through the rubble that used to be her neighbors' homes.
Photographer: Steve Schaefer

High tide swirls around the house that stood where Hugo cut a new channel through the island. What's left of the house is almost covered by the incoming tide. Photographer: Steve Schaefer

**Residents and rescue workers walk the beach among leaning power lines and debris.**
Photographer: Bryan Monroe

**David Ellerbe points to the water mark caused by Hugo's storm surge in the basement of his home. His home, built in 1893, sustained little damage, but several homes nearby were completely destroyed.**
Photographer: Steve Schaefer

**Uprooted palm trees lie amidst the broken-apart homes. On the southern end of Pawleys Island, a few houses, or what was left of them, were pushed against the mainland side of the creek.** Photographer: Charles Slate

**Walkways through the marsh were picked up
by Hugo and dumped on top of each other.**
Photographer: Charles Slate

**This view looks from the south end of
Pawleys Island, toward the Bird's Nest
section. More than half of the homes in the
Bird's Nest section were destroyed.**
Photographer: Charles Slate

"We've shed all the tears we can shed," said Jo Nell King, who had one of her Pawleys Island houses tossed across the street from its lot and a beachfront house in front of it survive untouched. "We want to try and get it back like it was as soon as we can." Reporter: Rebecca James

Among rubble and debris, Josephine Dean works her way in a raft across the newly formed channel on Pawleys Island. Residents formed a make-shift ferry service across the channel to carry homeowners to the southern tip of the island. Photographer: Bryan Monroe

**Durwood Perry surveys the damage to the porch of his summer home on the mainland of Pawleys Island. The porch is on the west side of his house. The front of his house, which faces the marsh, was almost completely gutted by water.** Photographer: Steve Schaefer

**Stamey J. Holland recovers a headboard, a family heirloom, from his beach house. The house was destroyed except for the fireplace.**
Photographer: Bryan Monroe

**Pawleys Island**

The contents of this house, broken apart by
wind, are scattered along the beach.
Photographer: Charles Slate

These yards on the north end of Pawleys
Island were filled with lumber and furniture.
Propane tanks were scattered everywhere.
Photographer: Charles Slate

Ellie Thomas holds up a newspaper from the day after Hurricane Hazel struck Myrtle Beach area in 1954. The paper washed up on Pawleys Island the day after Hurricane Hugo hit. "It still gives me goose bumps every time I look at it," she said. The picture in the paper was of the damage Pawleys Island suffered 25 years ago. Photographer: Steve Schaefer

**Remains of a wooden oceanfront bulkhead frame views of what's left of two neighboring houses.** Photographer: David Hill

A broken gate marks the entrance to an inlet walkway brushed by Hugo.
Photographer: Chris Germann

A bed frame was the only remaining piece of furniture at this oceanfront homesite.
Photographer: Charles Slate

A Pawleys Island family follows the trail of kitchen utensils to their home that Hugo tossed 250 yards back from the beach.
Photographer: Bryan Monroe

"We had more tide on this one than Hazel," said lifelong resident A.H. "Doc" Lachicotte as he surveyed the damage from across the creek in Pawleys Island. "It was 16 to 18 inches higher than Hazel, going by markings on my house." Reporter: David Hill

This small house on Pawleys Island was taken from its pilings, tossed across Doyle Avenue and came to rest in a yard across the street. Some homes were moved more than 100 yards from their original sites. Photographer: David Hill

**Jim and Clara Moore found their house number among the debris a block away from their home.** Photographer: Steve Schaefer

**Clara Moore surveys a pile of rubble that used to be her neighbor's home on the south side of Pawleys Island.** Photographer: Steve Schaefer

**Old Glory was jammed into the concrete foundation of a house on Pawleys Island, and was still waving after Hugo.** Photographer: Charles Slate

Bricks from a fireplace were the most easily recognized remains of a Pawleys Island beach house swept away by the Hugo storm surge estimated to have been 10 to 13 feet high.
Photographer: David Hill

"Tell everybody to have a little hope," said Mark Petree, who drove down from Winston-Salem, N.C., to check on his Pawleys Island vacation house. His house, formerly oceanfront, had been pushed north three lots and across the street from its foundation. Reporter: Rebecca James

"Our industry has never experienced a situation where we have had so much timber on the ground at one time," said Mack Singleton, president of Conway-based New South Inc. "For the short term, there will be a definite drop in value. In the long run, it will be higher because there will be less of it out there. It takes 30 years to grow a tree." Reporter: Ron Morrison

**Vivian Small's house in Litchfield was crushed by a tree.** Photographer: Bryan Monroe

**Aerial view of the Litchfield Inn.** Photographer:
Bill Scroggins

**Elaine McNeal records the
damage of Hurricane Hugo with
a camcorder while a bulldozer
pushes up debris in the street
behind her.** Photographer: Bill
Scroggins

Mike, Pat and Ann McNamara clean up the debris from Hurricane Hugo at the beach home of Ann and her husband Dr. James P. McNamara from Greenville, S.C. The high dunes — some 100 feet deep and 6 feet high — protected many of the oceanfront homes.
Photographer: Bill Scroggins

Restaurant chairs, benches, dock remnants and marsh grass filled the parking lot of the Outer Banks Seafood Co. restaurant.
Photographer: Barbara N. Heyward

"This is not what I had in mind a week ago, but you just have to roll with the punches," said Philip Wilkinson. He and Mary Mac were married in a 20-minute candlelight service at Belin Methodist Church in Murrells Inlet on Sept. 23. She wore black slacks and a checkered shirt, and Philip wore a khaki S.C. wildlife department uniform when they said "I do." "I brought my chain saw just in case we had to cut trees down to get over here." Reporter: Yolanda Jones

A porch rocker, sofa cushion and television were left in the yard debris of this house on Woodland in Murrells Inlet. Furnishings from homes in Garden City were swept across the creek and inlet and into yards in Murrells Inlet. Photographer: Barbara N. Heyward

Capt. Dick's Marina docks were destroyed and the building severely damaged. Photographer: Barbara N. Heyward

"Hey, not to worry," said author Mickey Spillane. First editions of his books, including "I, The Jury" and "My Gun Is Quick," had been swept from his Murrells Inlet home by Hurricane Hugo. So had some prized oil paintings of book covers, wedding pictures and three-fourths of his new manuscript. "The missing manuscript? Aw, no big deal. I'll make it up in two weeks. Two weeks, maybe three, that's how long it takes to write a book." Reporter: Mel Derrick

An aerial view of the damage done to Voyagers View Marina and Restaurant in Murrells Inlet. Photographer: Bill Scroggins

The creek side of the Ol' Shrimp Boat Restaurant was gutted by water. The boat is part of the restaurant and was not washed into the building. At least five restaurants had extensive damage. Photographer: Barbara N. Heyward.

**Sp-4 David Hobbs, with the 133rd MP Company of the S.C. National Guard from Timmonsville, waves to a car from his post barring traffic into Murrells Inlet.** Photographer: Bill Scroggins

Mystery writer Mickey Spillane and his wife, Jane, examine some of the many books that were destroyed by Hugo. First editions of his works and many copies in foreign languages were water-soaked when the water surge flooded their home. Photographer: Bill Scroggins

**Paula Wilson (left) and Loretta Small, co-workers at Nance's restaurant, comfort each other after surveying Hugo's damage to their place of employment.** Photographer: Steve Schaefer

Some boats, like the Capt. Bill and the New Capt. Bill, rode out Hugo up a creek off the Intracoastal Waterway, near Wacca Wache Marina.
Photographer: Bill Scroggins

**Utility lines along U.S. 17 Business were knocked into the road.** Photographer: Barbara N. Heyward

**"It won't be much of a honeymoon because we will spend it getting the tree off the roof of my house,"** said Philip Wilkinson, who got married the day after Hugo hit.
Reporter: Yolanda Jones

**The Dockside Restaurant's roof was damaged, and debris from Garden City blew across the inlet and into the restaurant's creek side.**
Photographer: Bill Scroggins

**David Michaux points to the hand-painted writing on the lid of an old, wooden trousseau trunk he found in his Murrells Inlet yard. The chest, a family heirloom, had been in a Garden City beach home and was washed 5 miles south by the Hugo's flood waters. Dorothy Hunter of Florence reclaimed her mother's hope chest.**
Photographer: Chris Germann

**"Trees get brittle as they get older, like people. The young trees did okay; the older ones took a beating,"** said Gurdon Tarbox, **director of Brookgreen Gardens.** Reporter: Caroline McDonald

**Saint Christopher, a bronze sculpture by Eleanore Melton on display at Brookgreen Gardens, was replaced on its pedestal after being knocked to the ground.** Photographer: Bill Scroggins

**An aerial view of the destruction in Garden City, looking south.** Photographer: Bill Scroggins

"You remember what you told us?" Mira Ajrulahi asked Lt. Phillip Thompson of the Horry County Police Department. Thompson nodded. "You told us, you were praying for us," the Garden City resident who wouldn't evacuate said. "At 2 o'clock in the morning, while the storm was going on, you were praying for us." The Ajrulahis had the Water's Edge Resort gift shop valuables in a 3,000-pound safe. The force of the water surge ripped the safe out of its concrete foundation, through a parking garage and across the street, over 100 feet away. Reporter: Mel Derrick

**"It's just totally destroyed,"** said Horry County Administrator M.L. Love, who inspected Garden City Friday morning with members of the National Guard. **"There is no front row. There's some pilings sticking up, that's about it."** Reporter: Bob Kudelka

**Walkways across the creek in the Mt. Gilead section of Garden City were piled on top of each other.** Photographer: Monty Cook

Randy Alford recovers a stuffed rabbit from a Waccamaw Drive home. Randy and Michael Alford (center) and Glenn Broach were cleaning up the remaining items of the beachfront home.
Photographer: Cecelia Konyn

**The Kingfisher Pier and Arcade after Hugo.**
Photographer: Cecelia Konyn

**The pier and arcade before Hugo.**
Photographer: Cecelia Konyn

**A Garden City man looks over some belongings in a Waccamaw Drive home that was hit hard by Hugo.** Photographer: Cecelia Konyn

**This Virginia car was hurled into a pile of rubble on Waccamaw Drive.** Photographer: Bill Scroggins

**Murrells Inlet-Garden City Fire Chief Terry Smith walks by one of the houses that was pushed into the middle of Waccamaw Drive on the south end of Garden City.**
Photographer: Bill Scroggins

**Work continued along Waccamaw Drive to restore power and telephone service to Garden City. So much ocean sand covered the street that bulldozers had to push it several feet high on each side of the road.**
Photographer: Steve Schaefer

Nine days after Sept. 21, Gordon Harris, Horry County Police Department chief, made it back to his double-wide home at the Garden City Mobile Home Resort on Murrells Inlet Creek. Everything was gone, trashed by Hurricane Hugo. "I just picked up (my) tackle box and (my son's water slide), and walked away. Went back to work. I had too many other things on my mind to be concerned about my losses."
Reporter: Mel Derrick

Power lines and poles were pushed over and onto houses by the storm surge.
Photographer: Bill Scroggins

**The wall is gone, the floor is sagging, but the phone sits neatly atop the phone book and the beds are still made in this Garden City home after the hurricane.** Photographer: Cecelia Konyn

"I started over after Hazel, and two years after Hazel I bought The Ship's Log, and four days after I bought it, a tornado flattened it, and I rebuilt, and now Hugo," said Paul Patrick, owner of Garden City Pier. "I'm older now, and don't know if I can rebuild again, a third time," he said as he walked through the remaining rubble of the pier with his son, David. Reporter: Cecelia Konyn

Waccamaw Drive was in ruins. About 100 homes were destroyed on Garden City Point, a fire official estimated. Water went as far as one-half mile back from the ocean. On the third row of houses near the pier, it was as high as 6 feet, judging from water marks. Photographer: Chris Germann

Sam's Corner, a popular spot for locals and tourists, is not much more than a shell. Owners Sam and Tim Baker are unsure what their plans are for rebuilding.
Photographer: Steve Schaefer

This home was smashed on Garden City Point.
Photographer: Bill Scroggins

"This is mild compared to south of here," said Horry County Administrator M.L. Love, of Waccamaw Drive in Garden City. The road was covered with sand and littered with air conditioners, toilets, water pipes and a stainless steel sink. A car jutted upward at a 45-degree angle as if driven into the sand. Reporter: Gil Thelen

An unidentified man videotapes the damage to an oceanfront motel in Garden City.
Photographer: Bryan Monroe

**Bulldozers roll along Garden City beach to help the cleanup efforts.** Photographer: Cecelia Konyn

**Firefighters from Murrells Inlet-Garden City Fire Department keep watch on one of several houses they burned in Garden City. The homeowners requested that the houses, which were destroyed by Hugo, be burned.** Photographer: Bill Scroggins

"The governor has taken a lot of flak for (keeping people from crossing to the beach side of the waterway)," said Gordon Harris, chief of the Horry County Police Department. "But a lot of us were involved in that decision. I was one of them. I'd been on the beachfront at Surfside and Garden City. I'd seen the destruction. The smell of propane gas was so strong you could hardly breathe. The power wires were down. We didn't know how many of them were hot. It simply wasn't safe. And we didn't want anyone getting hurt." Reporter: Mel Derrick

The addresses — 32 Dogwood and 32 Waccamaw — were two blocks apart, but the houses sit side by side after Hurricane Hugo. Photographer: Steve Schaefer

**"If we had tried to ride it out, we'd be dead. Our motel is now an oceanfront parking lot," said Gary Blake, owner of The Journey's End motel in Garden City.**

Reporter: Gil Thelen

A pier was driven into Dick Skillman's Magnolia Street home, damaging it. The Ocean View Motel, which Skillman has owned for 33 years, was also damaged by a part of Kingfisher Pier. Photographer: Cecelia Konyn

A couple check on the damage done to their uncle's house. Photographer: Cecelia Konyn

Debris litters the creek on the inlet side of the point in Garden City, one of the areas hardest hit by Hugo's powerful storm surge. Much of what was built facing the ocean had been pushed westward into the inlet.
Photographer: Bill Scroggins

Dee Madden is looking for a place to live and a job. Hurricane Hugo destroyed her bottom-floor apartment in Garden City. The storm took everything except her two children. "We had six feet of water in our house — mud and seaweed and everything else that comes from the ocean," said Madden, who worked at an oceanfront condominium building damaged by the hurricane. I have no income because my job is in the ocean, too." Reporter: Lesia J. Shannon

**Waccamaw Drive was washed out.**
Photographer: Bryan Monroe

Hugo's storm surge swept this home from its oceanfront lot into the middle of Ocean Boulevard. The random cruelty of Hurricane Hugo was evident in Surfside Beach. Some oceanfront houses were flattened while neighboring houses were left intact.
Photographer: Bill Scroggins

**"This is so massive. I've never seen anything like it before, and I hope I never do again."**
**Gov. Carroll Campbell.** Reporter: Chrysti Edge

**"What can you do? It's better than crying,"** said Cater Floyd, who joked as he talked about his destroyed Surfside Beach home.
Reporter: Lisa Greene

**Emergency vehicles travel along a flooded Ocean Boulevard three days after Hugo. In addition to a heavy rain that day, most of the south end of Surfside Beach was closed off because of live power lines.** Photographer: Cecelia Konyn

**Homes were turned to splinters along Ocean Boulevard in Surfside Beach.** Photographer: Cecelia Konyn

"I'll never leave again," said Gay Perry, owner of Perry Court in Myrtle Beach, after S.C. Troopers would not let her back across the Intracoastal Waterway Friday morning. "It's not right. We left (Myrtle Beach) because they (her family and police that came by her door) told us we could get back in in the morning." Reporter: Sammy Fretwell

Gary Bard sits on his front porch, resting after trying to find some of the clothes left in his apartment on Ocean Boulevard during Hugo. He hung the clothes any place he could find to get them to dry out.
Photographer: Cecelia Konyn

**Aerial view of a campground.** Photographer:
Bill Scroggins

"It's hard for me to remember what it
looked like before." Briarcliffe Acres
resident R.D. Garrell about the Grand
Strand's beachfront and sand dunes.
Reporter: Chrysti Edge

"My wife (Mary Emily) told me, 'Twenty years ago when we built Ocean Lakes, we didn't know what we were doing. Now the Good Lord has given us the opportunity to rebuild with 20 years experience,' " said Nelson Jackson, businessman and builder. He figures his properties, which include Ocean Lakes Family Campground and Prestwick Golf Course, suffered $4 million in damage from Hugo. Reporter: Mel Derrick

**Hugo rammed homes into each other at this campground, yet left many picnic shelters untouched.** Photographer: Bill Scroggins

Annette Heath (left) and Shea Hanner, once neighbors at Ocean Lakes Campground, stand near where their homes once stood.
Photographer: Steve Schaefer

Brothers Phil and Robert Newsome and neighbor Kevin Creach look out the destroyed bottom floor of their father's beach house, which they helped build. Photographer: Cecelia Konyn

**A wash-away pool at a Surfside Beach motel.** Photographer: Cecelia Konyn

**"It washed away the same way in Hazel,"** **said Cater Floyd of his uninsured Surfside** **Beach house. "It was put back then, but it** **won't be put back anymore."** Reporter: Lisa Greene

Hugo was moving a little faster than the posted speed limit on Ocean Boulevard, as both the smashed house in the background and the nearly buried speed limit sign attest. Photographer: Charles Slate

**Downed power lines at the Surfside Beach pier.** Photographer: Cecelia Konyn

**Old World War II target platforms in Long Bay Estates had been buried for years under several feet of sand dunes. Hugo's storm surge dug them out.** Photographer: Bryan Monroe

"It will be many, many months before things will get back to these families, before they will have a place to live, before they have some semblance of normalcy," said American Red Cross director Ron Ward of the people who have lost homes to Hugo.

Reporter: Lisa Greene

**Abner Fortner Jr. clears wood from his backyard after Hurricane Hugo came through.** Photographer: Bryan Monroe

**Irene Rolfe shows where water and debris blew through her home. She had just spent $50,000 renovating her Long Bay home.** Photographer: Bryan Monroe

Sitting on the porch railing, Abner Fortner Jr. points to where the oceanfront homes once stood in Long Bay Estates. Hugo's storm surge wiped away the home, but left the garage, right across the street. Photographer: Bryan Monroe

"I can't find my house," said Linda Williams as she walked through the debris at Long Bay Estates Sunday afternoon, looking for what used to be her home. "I think it's here, no over here, yeah, here . . . and there, and over there." The Williams' oceanfront home just south of Myrtle Beach was missing. Parts of it were in the trees. The roof was in a neighbor's yard. Nothing was left intact. Reporter: Bryan Monroe

Jenny Tisdale was a tenant in this beachfront house on Ocean Boulevard in Long Bay Estates, south of Myrtle Beach, until Hugo demolished it. "Everything's gone," she said. "I didn't take anything; thought it would turn and go away." Photographer: Bryan Monroe

**"I never in my wildest dreams imagined water could do all this,"** said Irene Rolfe of Long Bay Estates. **She had redecorated her home just three months earlier.** Reporter: Bryan Monroe

**Opal Allen and Lucas Williams, 1 year old, look at what's left of a house.** Photographer: Bryan Monroe

This view is of Myrtle Beach, looking north from the roof of the Regency Towers, at 2511 S. Ocean Blvd. High-rise hotels remained virtually intact, but swimming pools, first-floor lobbies, restaurants and parking lots were damaged. Photographer: Bill Scroggins

**Condo owners and friends look over the destruction caused by Hurricane Hugo in Myrtle Beach.** Photographer: Chris Germann

**The storm surge left the Myrtle Beach oceanfront torn and battered, as evidenced in this scene from the beach near 10th Avenue South.** Photographer: Steve Schaefer

Motel operators cleaned out damaged furnishings in an effort to get their businesses back open. This was the scene on the 2800 block of South Ocean Boulevard a few days after Hugo's visit. Photographer: Bill Scroggins

"That sand was the first line of defense," said Myrtle Beach innkeeper Vernon Brake. "It (Hugo) washed away our front lawn and started to undermine the pool decking (at the Breakers Resort). But (the renourishment sand) was right there. It slowed it down." He's convinced the $4.5 million worth of sand Myrtle Beach spread along the beaches in 1987 was worth every cent it cost. Reporter: Lisa Greene

This is an aerial view of the beach from the
Regency Towers, near 26th Avenue South.
According to S.C. Coastal Council estimates,
Myrtle Beach lost four to six feet of sand to
**Hugo.** Photographer: Bill Scroggins

"It was definitely a relative of hers, I can tell you that," said Earl Husted, who has run the Myrtle Beach Pavilion for more than four decades, comparing Hugo to Hurricane Hazel. Reporter: Joseph J. Serwach

**Springmaid Pier (foreground) was damaged extensively, as was Myrtle Beach State Park Pier.** Photographer: Bill Scroggins

"It looked like the end of the world to me," Jim Quattlebaum, business administrator for the First United Methodist Church, said of the steeple that fell into their sanctuary. "It was a very sad experience to see it. . . one of those things you don't like to see anywhere, especially in a place where you worship." Reporter: Caroline McDonald

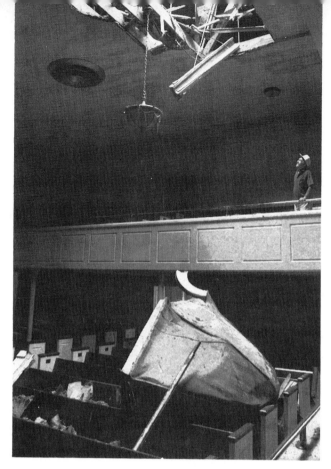

The Rev. Robert J. "Bob" Howell, pastor of First Methodist Church in Myrtle Beach, looks over damage to the sanctuary at 901 N. Kings Highway. The church's steeple went crashing through the roof and into the sanctuary. Photographer: Bill Scroggins

Workers remove the steeple from the First Methodist Church in Myrtle Beach after Hugo toppled it. Photographer: Bill Scroggins

Hugo crumpled the cement sidewalk between shops and the ocean. This shot was taken in front of Wings. Photographer: Steve Schaefer

"We will not give passes to sightseers and out-of-towners who have no business being in town," said Myrtle Beach City Manager Tom Leath about keeping people off the beach who came to see the devastation.
Reporter: Lesia J. Shannon

This picture looks north along The Myrtle Beach Pavilion boardwalk. Hurricane damage in Horry County is estimated at more than $600 million.
Photographer: Cecelia Konyn

**Glenn Harmon sprays the bottom of the swimming pool at the Breakers Hotel on Ocean Boulevard in Myrtle Beach. He was digging chairs out of the muck dumped into the pool.** Photographer: Chris Germann

**Mike Johnston (left) moves an electrical line so Wendel Ball can move debris behind the Poindexter Resort Inn at 17th Avenue North and Ocean Boulevard.** Photographer: Bill Scroggins

**This fish was one of the smaller victims of Hugo's wrath.** Photographer: Bryan Monroe

**Repair work begins on the ocean side of the Pavilion boardwalk.** Photographer: Cecelia Konyn

**PFC David Clark of the 51st Military Police Battalion of Florence waits for the replacement unit so he can go home. "After five long nights, you can put me down as ready to go home," he said.** Photographer: Cecelia Konyn

"It was pitch black and was worse than an eclipse. As the wind whirled around, it sounded like trains coming straight for me. It was something I will never forget," said Amos Johnson, who rode out the storm at the Lancer Motel in Myrtle Beach. Reporter: Yolanda Jones

James Wilson (left) shows Angelo Lary the deep hole left when winds uprooted this tree, destroying the sidewalk he had built at his house just eight days before. Several other trees landed on his house, damaging his Dunbar Street residence. Photographer: Charles Slate

**Craig Thomson looks as if he's getting help from the "Junk Sculpture" people while mopping in front of Ripley's Museum at the corner of Ninth Avenue North and Ocean Boulevard after Hugo passed through.** Photographer: Bill Scroggins

Horry County Fire Chief Hamp Shuping (front) and Stewart Pabst, assistant director and curator of the Horry County Museum, look over a large piece of a shipwreck uncovered by Hugo in the 81st Avenue North area of Myrtle Beach. Archeology experts say the beams and timbers are of a 19th-century ship. The remains could be part of the Freda A. Wiley, a Boston lumber ship that wrecked on the way to New Orleans during the Great Storm of 1898 and was uncovered by Hurricane Hazel at 43rd Avenue North in Myrtle Beach. Photographer: Cecelia Konyn

A piece of shipwreck discovered in the 81st Avenue North area of Myrtle Beach. Photographer: Cecelia Konyn

**The Second Avenue Pier, before Hugo.**
Photographer: Wendy Hilts

**Remnants of the Second Avenue Pier, after Hugo.** Photographer: Wendy Hilts

**Decking, parking lots and pools were jumbled
together along the Myrtle Beach oceanfront.**
Photographer: Steve Schaefer

Workers repair the damage caused by Hugo in the 2500 block of South Ocean Boulevard. Hugo's storm surge in Myrtle Beach was estimated at 15 to 17 feet, and its wind speed was clocked at 75 miles an hour. Photographer: Bill Scroggins

A tree lies in a sand trap on the 15th fairway at Heron Point golf course. Most Grand Strand courses suffered tree damage but opened up for play very quickly. Photographer: Charles Slate

"I think it's sick. I just hope they can put it back the way it was in Myrtle Beach instead of a disaster area." Bill Veasey, a worker at McAdoo's, 211 South Ocean Blvd., said of the way the city looked following Hurricane Hugo. Reporter: Lesia J. Shannon

This view looks south along the Shore Drive beach, minus its sand dune and oceanfront amenities. The areas dunes were destroyed and sand covered Shore Drive. At right is Pelican's Landing; at left is Pelican's Watch.
Photographer: Cynthia Struby

**A cracked pool at A Place At The Beach on Shore Drive. At least nine oceanfront swimming pools were destroyed and many others were damaged by tides that washed through buildings.** Photographer: Bill Scroggins

The Sands Ocean Club spa area after several weeks of clean-up. Both the ocean-front health club and restaurant were destroyed by tides. Photographer: Bill Scroggins

The seawall was left exposed along the oceanfront at Sands Beach Club.
Photographer: Bill Scroggins

**Repair work has been started at Sands Beach Club units that face the marsh.** Photographer: Bill Scroggins

**Before Hugo: The Holiday Inn fishing pier.**
Photographer: Bill Heath

**Holiday Inn fishing pier after Hugo.**
Photographer: Bill Heath

**"This is almost — not quite but almost — overwhelming," said North Myrtle Beach City Manager Bill Moss at daybreak Friday, surveying the storm damage.** Reporter: Chrysti Edge

**Peter Brusky surveys the damage to the sea wall and beach at the Windjammer Motel on Ocean Boulevard in North Myrtle Beach.**
Photographer: Steve Schaefer

**Gene Pennywitt gathers up a large sack of debris from his yard on Turner Street in North Myrtle Beach.** Photographer: Steve Schaefer

**North Myrtle Beach public safety officers, Billy Housare and Chris Baille, inform walkers that the beach is still closed.** Photographer: Steve Schaefer

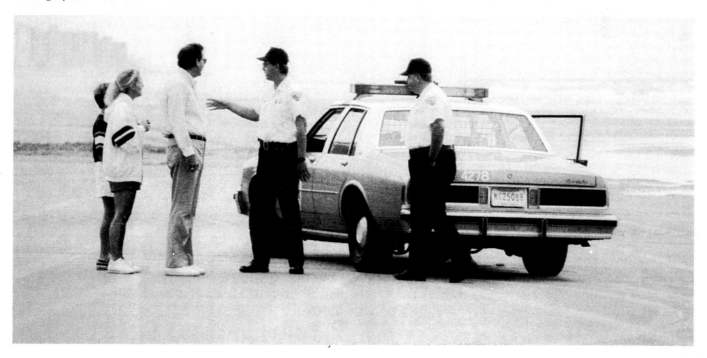

**Betty Jones, owner of the Shore Crest Motel, surveys the damage.** Photographer: Steve Schaefer

"Go ahead, make me a widow," said Julie Coy of North Myrtle Beach, when her husband, Kevin, left to walk on the beach just after Hurricane Hugo swept through. When he got back to the house, "he made us sleep in the closet," she said. Reporter: Chris Germann

**"(Hurricane) Hazel washed the first one away,"** . . . but **"I came right back. I said, 'Heck fire. You only live once,' "** said **Lexington, N.C., resident Bill Welborn as he surveyed the damage to his Cherry Grove home, "Hazel's Child."** Reporter: Chrysti Edge

**Residents weave around rubble as they try to reach their Cherry Grove homes.**
Photographer: Charles Slate

These oceanfront homes in the Cherry Grove
section of North Myrtle Beach suffered
extensive damage to their first floors, and all
the sand was washed away from the seawall.
Photographer: Charles Slate

"The pleasure that this has given us and all
those who have rented from us is just
something money can't buy," said R.W.
McManus, talking about his damaged
Cherry Grove home. Reporter: Chrysti Edge

**North Myrtle Beach City Manager Bill Moss saw fish jumping along Sea Mountain Highway about 3 a.m., four blocks from the ocean.** Reporter: Chrysti Edge

**These stairs stand all by themselves now on the beach in Cherry Grove. The home they were attached to was severed from them. The Cherry Grove section of North Myrtle Beach was one of the hardest hit areas along the Grand Strand.** Photographer: Charles Slate

**A beachfront home in Cherry Grove shows the signs of Hugo's wrath.** Photographer: Chris Germann

**Stuffed toy found alongside the road in Cherry Grove.**
Photographer: Charles Slate

**Front-end loaders removed sand from the road in the Cherry Grove section.**
Photographer: Charles Slate

**The road in the Cherry Grove section was covered with sand and debris.**
Photographer: Charles Slate

**A unidentified couple walk on the beach by the Cherry Grove pier the day after the hurricane hit.**
Photographer: Chris Germann

North Myrtle Beach

**"South Carolina is a poor state anyway,"** said Pete Bryant, former Sheraton employee and Myrtle Beach resident. "The last thing we needed was a hurricane."
Reporter: Caroline McDonald

North Myrtle Beach shelter volunteer Dick Blackburn takes a minute to sit down outside the shelter the day after Hugo. "I'm beat," he said. "But we're all safe, and that's what counts. There were some frayed nerves when the power went out, but the mood was really calm." Photographer: Chris Germann

**"Some people (who came to eat) had money, and some didn't. That didn't matter,"** Boots Jordan, owner of The Biscuit Shack in Cherry Grove said. **"What mattered was feeding people."** Reporter: Ettie Newlands

**These first-floor Cherry Grove motel rooms were destroyed as water swept away the beach, oceanfront amenities and the floor in this motel.** Photographer: Charles Slate

**The parking lot of the Cherry Grove Pier was
turned to rubble by the hurricane.**
Photographer: Steve Schaefer

**This shovel was found on the beach in the Cherry Grove section of North Myrtle Beach uncovered by winds and waves from Hurricane Hugo.** Photographer: Charles Slate

**Sofas litter the yard of this Cherry Grove condominium.** Photographer: Chris Germann

On Heron Circle, off Forestbrook Road, electric power was restored to all homes on that cul-de-sac except to the home of Betty and Charles Callahan. Mrs. Callahan, who is on a respirator 24 hours a day, could have been in serious trouble if it hadn't been for neighbor Ken Biddle. He ran an extension cord from his house to the Callahans. The extension cord worked until power was lost again in that area. Then Harold Morse, who lives across the street, took his 350-watt generator over to the Callahan house. Reporter: Mona Prufer

**The roof of Little River Traders lies in the front parking lot.** Photographer: Charles Slate

**"If people think they're alone in the dark, they're not,"** said Santee Cooper spokeswoman Jill Robbins, about downed electric lines. Reporter: Andrew Shain

**Tenth Avenue in Conway, like many Horry County streets west of the waterway, was a mass of debris and fallen power lines.** Photographer: Catherine Perkins Black

The pier at Sunset Beach, N.C., was severely damaged, and erosion was heavy, but most residences were spared by Hugo. Property damage was minimal because development followed setback laws and the beach is wide.
Photographer: Charles Slate

**The Rev. Henderson White loads donated
food and other necessities for hurricane relief
onto a pickup truck to take from Camp
Baskervill, in Pawleys Island, to the
Bloomingville Community Center, off S.C.
527.** Photographer: Chris Germann

"If you haven't taken a shower in a couple of days, please do so," said Myrtle Beach City spokesman Pat Dowling, after water conservation restraints were lifted. Reporter: Lisa Greene

Henry Dean changes the sign at J.B. Quick's in Socastee to let people know the business is open. Photographer: Charles Slate

Christy Padgett and her daughter Laura, 8, are assisted by Elaine James at the Ocean Lakes Campground office of the Red Cross. Photographer: Bill Scroggins

**Thanksgiving And Recovery**

**Long lines formed at the Horry County Social Services offices at 21st Avenue North as people applied for emergency food stamps.** Photographer: Chris Germann

**In Georgetown, a long, wide, patient line formed on Highmarket Street, all the way down a city block to Dozier Street as residents applied for emergency food stamp aid. Some folks reportedly had to wait as long as eight hours.** Photographer: Chris Germann

**"This is a helluva time to try to take advantage of somebody who's on his knees already. We're just not going to allow it to happen,"** said Myrtle Beach Mayor Bob Grissom, about price gouging. Reporter: Chrysti Edge

**Two-month-old Rochelle Vereen is surrounded by shoes at the Murrells Inlet Red Cross center.** Photographer: Cecelia Konyn

**Red Cross volunteers sort through the stacks of clothing and food donated to the relief effort at the collection center in the First Baptist Church on Third Avenue North in Myrtle Beach.** Photographer: Bryan Monroe

**Thanksgiving And Recovery**

**"Mother Nature will heal a lot of that,"** said Horry County extension agent Bill Witherspoon, about the damage from wind and salt spray to trees and foliage. Reporter: Mona Prufer

**Church services were held across the Grand Strand the Sunday after Hugo to pray for victims of the hurricane.** Photographer: Bill Scroggins

**"We need to let the world know we're OK,"** said J. Michael Pate, publisher of The Sun News and organizer of a task force of Grand Strand tourism officials and business owners. "Even though we've taken a pretty hard blow, we're still in business and we're still here." Reporter: Bob Kudelka

Visitors return to the beach after officials opened the northern part of oceanfront Myrtle Beach to the public. Here, about 14th Avenue North, beachcombers dodge the rubble and leftovers of Hurricane Hugo.
Photographer: Chris Germann

Thanksgiving And Recovery

A front-end loader pushes sand on the beach near Regency Towers in the 2500 block of Ocean Boulevard in preparation for mid-October's expected high tides. Photographer: Bill Scroggins

Bulldozers scrape sand up onto the dunes in the Litchfield Beach area. Photographer: Cecelia Konyn

**"I hate this curfew. We're losing a tremendous amount of business,"** said **Brian Helwagen, manager of G.D. Ritzy's in Myrtle Beach.** Reporter: Yolanda Jones

**Scottie Burgess gets ready for an uncurfew party at Mary Juel's restaurant, near 48th Avenue North in Myrtle Beach. The restaurant planned to celebrate the lifting of the curfew with happy hour and live music.** Photographer: Steve Schaefer

Front-end loaders are busy pushing sand back onto what was left of the dunes along Litchfield Beach. The effort was part of a renourishment project for Grand Strand beaches, which took a battering from **Hurricane Hugo.** Photographer: Steve Schaefer

"It was the moral and ethical thing to do. My God, you guys are in such terrible shape up there. There was no doubt this was something we had to do," said Hilton Head Town Councilman Bill Marscher, on giving back Coastal Council renourishment funds to help the damaged beachfront in Horry, Georgetown and Charleston counties.

Reporter: Sammy Fretwell

Women go through clothes at the Red Cross distribution center in the First Baptist Church in Myrtle Beach. Photographer: Bryan Monroe

**"Most of them are hungry," said Micky Dottie of Myrtle Beach. "There are a lot of people with a little meat that thawed that had to be thrown away. . . . They're standing in line (for food stamps) from 5 this morning."** Reporter: Caroline McDonald

A young girl is very happy with the new toy she picked out at the Murrells Inlet Red Cross center. Photographer: Cecelia Konyn

**The Rev. Bob Morris of Belin Methodist Church in Murrells Inlet greets churchgoers after Sunday service there.** Photographer: Bill Scroggins

Sandy Hall and Carol Blackstone of Mansfield, Ohio, sit on the beach in front of the Bel-Aire Motel in North Myrtle Beach where they were vacationing. "We're lounging by the pool — can't you tell?" said Hall. "They (Bel-Aire management) told us the pool was gone, but the rooms and the courtyard were perfect. We Ohioans, we're brave." Photographer: Chris Germann

"We're not a network station so we don't make a lot of money except donations. We don't get a lot of money. This is one way we can make some money," said Dave Dempsey, master control supervisor for WGSE-TV (43), about selling copies of tapes of Hurricane Hugo's damage the station broadcast. Reporter: David Hill

Two-year-old Stephen Blair of Conway is happy again. When Hugo blew away some of his toys, his mother, Pam, said he could have a puppy. He adopted two puppies from the Myrtle Beach Animal Shelter on 10th Avenue North.
Photographer: Cecelia Konyn

"My mother always said, 'Everything the good Lord does is for some reason.' It's hard to look at this destruction and see the purpose," said Gordon Harris, chief of the Horry County Police Department. "And yet, the spirit of cooperation after Hugo, this coming together of us all, maybe that's what the Lord wanted. Maybe He was trying to show us that we had our priorities wrong. Maybe He was telling us all, 'I'm going to help you get things right.'"

Reporter: Mel Derrick

# Where I was during Hurricane Hugo...

# My Hurricane Hugo pictures...

# My Hurricane Hugo pictures...

# My Hurricane Hugo pictures...

**breadbox** (US) n Brotkasten m;
**breadcrumbs** npl Brotkrumen pl; (Gastr)
Paniermehl nt; **breaded** adj paniert;
**breadknife** n Brotmesser nt
**breadth** [bredθ] n Breite f
**break** [breɪk] n (fracture) Bruch m; (rest)
Pause f; (short holiday) Kurzurlaub m; **give
me a ~** gib mir eine Chance, hör auf
damit! ▷ vt (**broke, broken**) (fracture)
brechen; (in pieces) zerbrechen; (toy, device)
kaputtmachen; (promise) nicht halten;
(silence) brechen; (law) verletzen; (journey)
unterbrechen; (news) mitteilen (to sb jdm);
**I broke my leg** ich habe mir das Bein
gebrochen; **he broke it to her gently** er
hat es ihr schonend beigebracht ▷ vi
(come apart) (auseinander) brechen; (in
pieces) zerbrechen; (toy, device)
kaputtgehen; (person) zusammenbrechen;
(day, dawn) anbrechen; (news) bekannt
werden; **break down** vi (car) eine Panne
haben; (machine) versagen; (person)
zusammenbrechen; **break in** vi (burglar)
einbrechen; **break into** vt einbrechen in
+akk; **break off** vi, vt abbrechen; **break
out** vi ausbrechen; **to ~ in a rash** einen
Ausschlag bekommen; **break up** vi
aufbrechen; (meeting, organisation) sich
auflösen; (marriage) in die Brüche gehen;
(couple) sich trennen; **school breaks up on
Friday** am Freitag beginnen die Ferien
▷ vt aufbrechen; (marriage) zerstören;
(meeting) auflösen; **breakable** adj
zerbrechlich; **breakage** n Bruch m;
**breakdown** n (of car) Panne f; (of machine)
Störung f; (of person, relations, system)
Zusammenbruch m; **breakdown service**
n Pannendienst m; **breakdown truck** n
Abschleppwagen m
**breakfast** ['brekfəst] n Frühstück nt; **to
have ~** frühstücken; **breakfast cereal** n
Cornflakes, Muesli etc; **breakfast television**
n Frühstücksfernsehen nt
**break-in** ['breɪkɪn] n Einbruch m;
**breakup** ['breɪkʌp] n (of meeting,
organization) Auflösung f; (of marriage)
Zerrüttung f
**breast** [brest] n Brust f; **breastfeed**
stillen; **breaststroke** n Brustschwimme
nt
**breath** [breθ] n Atem m; **out of ~** außer
Atem; **breathalyse, breathalyze**
['breθəlaɪz] vt (ins Röhrchen) blasen

lassen; **breathalyser, breathalyzer** n
Promillemesser m; **breathe** [bri:ð] vt, vi
atmen; **breathe in** vt, vi einatmen;
**breathe out** vt, vi ausatmen;
**breathless** ['breθlɪs] adj atemlos;
**breath-taking** ['breθteɪkɪŋ] adj
atemberaubend
**bred** [bred] pt, pp of **breed**
**breed** [bri:d] n (race) Rasse f ▷ vi (**bred,
bred**) sich vermehren ▷ vt züchten;
**breeder** n Züchter(in) m(f); (fam) Hetero
m; **breeding** n (of animals) Züchtung f; (of
person) (gute) Erziehung
**breeze** [bri:z] n Brise f
**brevity** ['brevɪtɪ] n Kürze f
**brew** [bru:] vt (beer) brauen; (tea) kochen;
**brewery** n Brauerei f
**bribe** ['braɪb] n Bestechungsgeld n ▷ vt
bestechen; **bribery** ['braɪbərɪ] n
Bestechung f
**brick** [brɪk] n Backstein m; **bricklayer** n
Maurer(in) m(f)
**bride** [braɪd] n Braut f; **bridegroom** n
Bräutigam m; **bridesmaid** n Brautjungfer
f
**bridge** [brɪdʒ] n Brücke f; (cards) Bridge nt
**brief** [bri:f] adj kurz ▷ vt instruieren (on
über +akk); **briefcase** n Aktentasche f;
**briefs** npl Slip m
**bright** [braɪt] adj hell; (colour) leu
(cheerful) heiter; (intelligent) inte
(idea) glänzend; **brighten up**
(person) aufheitern ▷ vi si
(person) fröhlicher wer
**brilliant** ['brɪljənt]
strahlend; (person)
glänzend; (Brit
fantastisch
**brim** [brɪ
**bring**
brin
a

**Brit** [brɪt] n (fam) Brite m, Britin f; **Britain** ['brɪtn] n Großbritannien nt; **British** ['brɪtɪʃ] adj britisch; **the ~ Isles** (pl) die Britischen Inseln pl ▷ n **the ~** (pl) die Briten pl

**Brittany** ['brɪtənɪ] n die Bretagne

**brittle** ['brɪtl] adj spröde

**broad** [brɔːd] adj breit; (accent) stark; **in ~ daylight** am helllichten Tag ▷ (US fam) Frau f

**B road** ['biːrəʊd] n (Brit) ≈ Landstraße f

**broadcast** ['brɔːdkɑːst] n Sendung f ▷ irr vt, vi senden; (event) übertragen

**broaden** ['brɔːdn] vt **to ~ the mind** den Horizont erweitern; **broad-minded** adj tolerant

**broccoli** ['brɒkəlɪ] n Brokkoli pl

**brochure** ['brəʊʃjʊə*] n Prospekt m, Broschüre f

**broke** [brəʊk] pt of **break** ▷ adj (Brit fam) pleite; **broken** ['brəʊkən] pp of **break**; **broken-hearted** adj untröstlich

**broker** ['brəʊkə*] n Makler(in) m(f)

**brolly** ['brɒlɪ] n (Brit fam) Schirm m

**bronchitis** [brɒŋ'kaɪtɪs] n Bronchitis f

**bronze** [brɒnz] n Bronze f

**brooch** [brəʊtʃ] n Brosche f

**broom** [bruːm] n Besen m

**Bros** [brɒs] abbr = **brothers** Gebr.

**broth** [brɒθ] n Fleischbrühe f

**brothel** ['brɒθl] n Bordell nt

**brother** ['brʌðə*] n Bruder m; **~s** (pl) (Comm) Gebrüder pl; **brother-in-law** (pl **brothers-in-law**) n Schwager m

**~ught** [brɔːt] pt, pp of **bring**

**~w** [braʊ] n (eyebrow) (Augen)braue f; ~head) Stirn f

[braʊn] adj braun; **brown bread** n rot nt; (wholemeal) Vollkornbrot nt; ~e ['braʊnɪ] n (Gastr) Brownie m; ~e Pfadfinderin; **brown paper** n r nt; **brown rice** n Naturreis m; ~ar n brauner Zucker

~z] vi (in book) blättern; (in ~ern, herumschauen; ~form) Browser m

blauer Fleck ▷ vt **to** dat einen blauen Fleck

n Brünette f e f; (for sweeping) ~nting) Pinsel m ▷ vt **to ~ one's teeth**

sich dat die Zähne putzen; **brush up** vt (French etc) auffrischen

**Brussels sprouts** [brʌsl'spraʊts] npl Rosenkohl m, Kohlsprossen pl

**brutal** ['bruːtl] adj brutal; **brutality** [bruː'tælɪtɪ] n Brutalität f

**BSE** abbr = **bovine spongiform encephalopathy** BSE f

**bubble** ['bʌbl] n Blase f; **bubble bath** n Schaumbad nt; **bubbly** ['bʌblɪ] adj sprudelnd; (person) temperamentvoll ▷ n (fam) Schampus m

**buck** [bʌk] n (animal) Bock m; (US fam) Dollar m

**bucket** ['bʌkɪt] n Eimer m

### Buckingham Palace

Der **Buckingham Palace** ist die offizielle Londoner Residenz der britischen Monarchen und liegt am St James's Park. Der Palast wurde 1703 für den Herzog von Buckingham erbaut, 1762 von George III gekauft, zwischen 1821 und 1836 von John Nash umgebaut, und Anfang des 20. Jahrhunderts teilweise neu gestaltet. Teile des Buckingham Palace sind heute der Öffentlichkeit zugänglich.

**buckle** ['bʌkl] n Schnalle f ▷ vi (Tech) sich verbiegen ▷ vt zuschnallen

**bud** [bʌd] n Knospe f

**Buddhism** ['bʊdɪzəm] n Buddhismus m; **Buddhist** adj buddhistisch ▷ n Buddhist(in) m(f)

**buddy** ['bʌdɪ] n (fam) Kumpel m

**budget** ['bʌdʒɪt] n Budget nt

**budgie** ['bʌdʒɪ] n (fam) Wellensittich m

**buff** [bʌf] adj (US) muskulös; **in the ~** nackt ▷ n (enthusiast) Fan m

**buffalo** ['bʌfələʊ] (pl **-es**) n Büffel m

**buffer** ['bʌfə*] n (a. Inform) Puffer m

**buffet** ['bʊfeɪ] n (food) (kaltes) Büfett nt

**bug** [bʌg] n (Inform) Bug m, Programmfehler m; (listening device) Wanze f; (US: insect) Insekt nt; (fam: illness) Infektion f ▷ vt (fam) nerven

**bugger** ['bʌgə*] n (vulg) Scheißkerl m ▷ interj (vulg) Scheiße f; **bugger off** vi (vulg) abhauen, Leine ziehen

**buggy®** ['bʌgɪ] n (for baby) Buggy® m; (US: pram) Kinderwagen m

**build** [bɪld] (**built, built**) vt bauen; **build up** vt aufbauen; **builder** n Bauunternehmer(in) m(f); **building** n Gebäude nt; **building site** n Baustelle f; **building society** n Bausparkasse f

**built** pt, pp of **build**; **built-in** adj (cupboard) Einbau-, eingebaut

**bulb** [bʌlb] n (Bot) (Blumen)zwiebel f; (Elec) Glühbirne f

**Bulgaria** [bʌlˈgeərɪə] n Bulgarien nt; **Bulgarian** adj bulgarisch ▷ n (person) Bulgare m, Bulgarin f; (language) Bulgarisch nt

**bulimia** [bəˈlɪmɪə] n Bulimie f

**bulk** [bʌlk] n (size) Größe f; (greater part) Großteil m (of +gen); **in ~** en gros; **bulky** adj (goods) sperrig; (person) stämmig

**bull** [bʊl] n Stier m; **bulldog** n Bulldogge f; **bulldoze** [ˈbʊldəʊz] vt planieren; **bulldozer** n Planierraupe f

**bullet** [ˈbʊlɪt] n Kugel f

**bulletin** [ˈbʊlɪtɪn] n Bulletin nt; (announcement) Bekanntmachung f; (Med) Krankenbericht m; **bulletin board** n (US: Inform) schwarzes Brett

**bullfight** [ˈbʊlfaɪt] n Stierkampf m; **bullshit** n (fam) Scheiß m

**bully** [ˈbʊlɪ] n Tyrann m

**bum** [bʌm] n (Brit fam: backside) Po m; (US: vagrant) Penner m; (worthless person) Rumtreiber m; **bum around** vi herumgammeln

**bumblebee** [ˈbʌmblbiː] n Hummel f

**bump** [bʌmp] n (fam: swelling) Beule f; (road) Unebenheit f; (blow) Stoß m ▷ vt stoßen; **to ~ one's head** sich dat den Kopf anschlagen (on an +dat); **bump into** vt stoßen gegen; (fam: meet) (zufällig) begegnen +dat; **bumper** n (Auto) Stoßstange f ▷ adj (edition etc) Riesen-; (crop etc) Rekord-; **bumpy** [ˈbʌmpɪ] adj holp(e)rig

**bun** [bʌn] n süßes Brötchen

**bunch** [bʌntʃ] n (of flowers) Strauß m; (fam: of people) Haufen m; **~ of keys** Schlüsselbund m; **~ of grapes** Weintraube f

**bundle** [ˈbʌndl] n Bündel nt

**bungalow** [ˈbʌŋgələʊ] n Bungalow m

**bungee jumping** [ˈbʌndʒɪdʒʌmpɪŋ] n Bungeejumping nt

**bunk** [bʌŋk] n Koje f; **bunk bed(s)** n(pl) Etagenbett nt

**bunker** [ˈbʌŋkə*] n (Mil) Bunker m

**bunny** [ˈbʌnɪ] n Häschen nt

**buoy** [bɔɪ] n Boje f; **buoyant** [ˈbɔɪənt] adj (floating) schwimmend

**BUPA** [ˈbuːpə] abbr (Brit) private Krankenkasse

**burden** [ˈbɜːdn] n Last f

**bureau** [ˈbjʊərəʊ] n Büro nt; (government department) Amt nt; **bureaucracy** [bjʊˈrɒkrəsɪ] n Bürokratie f; **bureaucratic** [bjuːrəˈkrætɪk] adj bürokratisch; **bureau de change** [ˈbjuːrəʊ də ˈʃɒnʒ] n Wechselstube f

**burger** [ˈbɜːgə*] n Hamburger m

**burglar** [ˈbɜːglə*] n Einbrecher(in) m(f); **burglar alarm** n Alarmanlage f; **burglarize** vt (US) einbrechen in +akk; **burglary** n Einbruch m; **burgle** [ˈbɜːgl] vt einbrechen in +akk

**burial** [ˈberɪəl] n Beerdigung f

**burn** [bɜːn] (**burnt** o **burned, burnt** o **burned**) vt verbrennen; (food, slightly) anbrennen; **to ~ one's hand** sich dat die Hand verbrennen ▷ vi brennen ▷ n (injury) Brandwunde f; (on material) verbrannte Stelle; **burn down** vt, vi abbrennen

**burp** [bɜːp] vi rülpsen ▷ vt (baby) aufstoßen lassen

**bursary** [ˈbɜːsərɪ] n Stipendium nt

**burst** [bɜːst] (**burst, burst**) vt platzen lassen ▷ vi platzen; **to ~ into tears** in Tränen ausbrechen

**bury** [ˈberɪ] vt begraben; (in grave) beerdigen; (hide) vergraben

**bus** [bʌs] n Bus m; **bus driver** n Busfahrer(in) m(f)

**bush** [bʊʃ] n Busch m

**business** [ˈbɪznɪs] n Geschäft nt; (enterprise) Unternehmen nt; (concern, affair) Sache f; **I'm here on ~** ich bin geschäftlich hier; **it's none of your ~** das geht dich nichts an; **business card** n Visitenkarte f; **business class** n (Aviat) Businessclass f; **business hours** npl Geschäftsstunden pl; **businessman** (pl **-men**) n Geschäftsmann m; **business studies** npl Betriebswirtschaftslehre f; **businesswoman** (pl **-women**) n Geschäftsfrau f

**bus service** n Busverbindung f; **bus shelter** n Wartehäuschen nt; **bus station** n Busbahnhof m; **bus stop** n Bushaltestelle f

**bust** [bʌst] n Büste f ▷ adj (broken) kaputt; **to go ~** Pleite gehen; **bust-up** n (fam) Krach m

**busy** ['bɪzɪ] adj beschäftigt; (street, place) belebt; (esp US: telephone) besetzt; **~ signal** (US) Besetztzeichen nt

 **KEYWORD**

**but** [bʌt] conj **1** (yet) aber; **not X but Y** nicht X sondern Y

**2** (however): **I'd love to come, but I'm busy** ich würde gern kommen, bin aber beschäftigt

**3** (showing disagreement, surprise etc): **but that's fantastic!** (aber) das ist ja fantastisch!

▷ prep (apart from, except); **nothing but trouble** nichts als Ärger; **no-one but him can do it** niemand außer ihn kann es machen; **but for you/your help** ohne dich/deine Hilfe; **anything but that** alles, nur das nicht

▷ adv (just, only); **she's but a child** sie ist noch ein Kind; **had I but known** wenn ich es nur gewusst hätte; **I can but try** ich kann es immerhin versuchen; **all but finished** so gut wie fertig

**butcher** ['bʊtʃə*] n Fleischer(in) m(f), Metzger(in) m(f)

**butler** ['bʌtlə*] n Butler m

**butter** ['bʌtə*] n Butter f ▷ vt buttern; **buttercup** n Butterblume f; **butterfly** n Schmetterling m

**buttocks** ['bʌtəks] npl Gesäß nt

**button** ['bʌtn] n Knopf m; (badge) Button m ▷ vt zuknöpfen; **buttonhole** n Knopfloch m

**buy** [baɪ] n Kauf m ▷ vt (bought, bought) kaufen; (from von); **he bought me a ring** er hat mir einen Ring gekauft; **buyer** n Käufer(in) m(f)

**buzz** [bʌz] n Summen nt; **to give sb a ~** (fam) jdn anrufen ▷ vi summen; **buzzer** ['bʌzə*] n Summer m; **buzz word** n (fam) Modewort nt

 **KEYWORD**

**by** [baɪ] prep **1** (referring to cause, agent) von durch; **killed by lightning** vom Blitz getötet; **a painting by Picasso** ein Gemälde von Picasso

**2** (referring to method, manner): **by bus/car/train** mit dem Bus/Auto/Zug; **to pay by cheque** per Scheck bezahlen; **by moonlight** bei Mondschein; **by saving hard, he ...** indem er eisern sparte, ... er ...

**3** (via, through) über +acc; **he came in by the back door** er kam durch die Hintertür herein

**4** (close to, past) bei an +dat; **a holiday by the sea** ein Urlaub am Meer; **she rushed by me** sie eilte an mir vorbei

**5** (not later than): **by 4 o'clock** bis 4 Uhr: **by this time tomorrow** morgen um diese Zeit; **by the time I got here it was too late** als ich hier ankam, war es zu spät

**6** (during): **by day** bei Tag

**7** (amount): **by the kilo/metre** kiloweise/meterweise; **paid by the hour** stundenweise bezahlt

**8** (Math, measure): **to divide by 3** durch 3 teilen; **to multiply by 3** mit 3 malnehmen; **a room 3 metres by 4** ein Zimmer 3 mal 4 Meter; **it's broader by a metre** es ist (um) einem Meter breiter

**9** (according to) nach; **it's all right by me** von mir aus gern

**10**: (all) **by oneself** etc ganz allein

**11**: **by the way** übrigens

▷ adv **1**: see **go, pass** etc

**2**: **by and by** irgendwann; (with past tenses) nach einiger Zeit; **by and large** (on the whole) im Großen und Ganzen

**bye-bye** ['baɪ'baɪ] interj (fam) Wiedersehen, tschüss

**by-election** n Nachwahl f; **bypass** n Umgehungsstraße f; (Med) Bypass m; **byproduct** n Nebenprodukt nt; **byroad** n Nebenstraße f; **bystander** n Zuschauer(in) m(f)

**byte** [baɪt] n Byte nt

# C

**C** [siː] abbr = **Celsius** C

**c** abbr = **circa** ca

**cab** [kæb] n Taxi nt

**cabbage** ['kæbɪdʒ] n Kohl m

**cabin** ['kæbɪn] n (Naut) Kajüte f; (Aviat) Passagierraum m; (wooden house) Hütte f; **cabin crew** n Flugbegleitpersonal nt; **cabin cruiser** n Kajütboot nt

**cabinet** ['kæbɪnɪt] n Schrank m; (for display) Vitrine f; (Pol) Kabinett nt

**cable** ['keɪbl] n (Elec) Kabel nt; **cable-car** n Seilbahn f; **cable railway** n Drahtseilbahn f; **cable television**, **cablevision** (US) n Kabelfernsehen nt

**cactus** ['kæktəs] n Kaktus m

**CAD** abbr = **computer-aided design** CAD nt

**Caesarean** [siː'zɛərɪən] adj ~ (**section**) Kaiserschnitt m

**café** ['kæfeɪ] n Café nt; **cafeteria** [kæfɪ'tɪərɪə] n Cafeteria f; **cafetiere** [kæfə'tjɛə*] n Kaffeebereiter m

**caffein(e)** ['kæfiːn] n Koffein nt

**cage** [keɪdʒ] n Käfig m

**Cairo** ['kaɪərəʊ] n Kairo nt

**cake** [keɪk] n Kuchen m; **cake shop** n Konditorei f

**calamity** [kə'læmɪtɪ] n Katastrophe f

**calculate** ['kælkjʊleɪt] vt berechnen; (estimate) kalkulieren; **calculating** adj berechnend; **calculation** [kælkjʊ'leɪʃən] n Berechnung f; (estimate) Kalkulation f; **calculator** ['kælkjʊleɪtə*] n Taschenrechner m

**calendar** ['kælɪndə*] n Kalender m

**calf** [kɑːf] (pl **calves**) n Kalb nt; (Anat) Wade f

**California** [kælɪ'fɔːnɪə] n Kalifornien nt

**call** [kɔːl] vt rufen; (name, describe as) nennen; (Tel) anrufen; (Inform, Aviat) aufrufen; **what's this ~ed?** wie heißt das?; **that's what I ~ service** das nenne ich guten Service ▷ vi (shout) rufen (for help um Hilfe); (visit) vorbeikommen; **to ~ at the doctor's** beim Arzt vorbeigehen; (of train) **to ~ at ... in ...** halten ▷ n (shout) Ruf m; (Tel) Anruf; (Inform, Aviat) Aufruf m; **to make a ~** telefonieren; **to give sb a ~** jdn anrufen; **to be on ~** Bereitschaftsdienst haben; **call back** vt, vi zurückrufen; **call for** vt (come to pick up) abholen; (demand, require) verlangen; **call off** vt absagen

**call centre** n Callcenter nt; **caller** n Besucher(in) m(f); (Tel) Anrufer(in) m(f)

**calm** [kɑːm] n Stille f; (also of person) Ruhe f; (of sea) Flaute f ▷ vt beruhigen ▷ adj ruhig; **calm down** vi, vt sich beruhigen

**calorie** ['kælərɪ] n Kalorie f

**calves** [kɑːvz] pl of **calf**

**Cambodia** [kæm'bəʊdɪə] n Kambodscha nt

**camcorder** ['kæmkɔːdə*] n Camcorder m

**came** [keɪm] pt of **come**

**camel** ['kæməl] n Kamel nt

**camera** ['kæmərə] n Fotoapparat m, Kamera f

**camomile** ['kæməmaɪl] n Kamille f

**camouflage** ['kæməflɑːʒ] n Tarnung f

**camp** [kæmp] n Lager nt; (camping place) Zeltplatz m ▷ vi zelten, campen ▷ adj (fam) theatralisch, tuntig

**campaign** [kæm'peɪn] n Kampagne f; (Pol) Wahlkampf m ▷ vi sich einsetzen (for/against für/gegen)

**campbed** ['kæmpbed] n Campingliege f; **camper** ['kæmpə*] n (person) Camper(in) m(f); (van) Wohnmobil nt; **camping** ['kæmpɪŋ] n Zelten nt, Camping nt; **campsite** ['kæmpsaɪt] n Zeltplatz m, Campingplatz m

**campus** [ˈkæmpəs] n (of university)
Universitätsgelände nt, Campus m
**can¹** [kæn] (**could, been able**) vb aux (be
able) können; (permission) dürfen; **I ~not** o
**~'t see** ich kann nichts sehen; **~ I go now?**
darf ich jetzt gehen? ▷ n (for food, beer)
Dose f; (for water, milk) Kanne f

**KEYWORD**

**can²** [kæn] (negative **cannot, can't**,
conditional **could**) aux vb **1** (be able to, know
how to) können; **I can see you tomorrow,
if you like** ich könnte Sie morgen sehen,
wenn Sie wollen; **I can swim** ich kann
schwimmen; **can you speak German?**
sprechen Sie Deutsch?
**2** (may) können dürfen; **could I have a
word with you?** könnte ich Sie kurz
sprechen?

**Canada** [ˈkænədə] n Kanada nt;
**Canadian** [kəˈneɪdjən] adj kanadisch ▷ n
Kanadier(in) m(f)
**canal** [kəˈnæl] n Kanal m
**canary** [kəˈnɛərɪ] n Kanarienvogel m
**cancel** [ˈkænsəl] vt (plans) aufgeben;
(meeting, event) absagen; (Comm: order etc)
stornieren; (contract) kündigen; (Inform)
löschen; (Aviat: flight) streichen; **to be ~led**
(event, train, bus) ausfallen; **cancellation**
[kænsəˈleɪʃən] n Absage f; (Comm)
Stornierung f; (Aviat) gestrichener Flug
**cancer** [ˈkænsə*] n (Med) Krebs m; **Cancer**
n (Astr) Krebs m
**candid** [ˈkændɪd] adj (person, conversation)
offen
**candidate** [ˈkændɪdət] n (for post)
Bewerber(in) m(f); (Pol) Kandidat(in) m(f)
**candle** [ˈkændl] n Kerze f; **candlelight** n
Kerzenlicht nt; **candlestick** n
Kerzenhalter m
**candy** [ˈkændɪ] n (US) Bonbon nt;
(quantity) Süßigkeiten pl; **candy-floss** n
(Brit) Zuckerwatte f
**cane** [keɪn] n Rohr nt; (stick) Stock
m
**cannabis** [ˈkænəbɪs] n Cannabis m
**canned** [kænd] adj Dosen-
**cannot** [ˈkænɒt] contr of **can not**
**canny** [ˈkænɪ] adj (shrewd) schlau
**canoe** [kəˈnuː] n Kanu nt; **canoeing** n
Kanufahren nt

**canopener** [ˈkænəʊpnə*] n Dosenöffner m
**canopy** [ˈkænəpɪ] n Baldachin m; (awning)
Markise f; (over entrance) Vordach nt
**can't** [kɑːnt] contr of **can not**
**canteen** [kænˈtiːn] n (in factory) Kantine
f; (in university) Mensa f
**canvas** [ˈkænvəs] n (for sails, shoes)
Segeltuch nt; (for tent) Zeltstoff m; (for
painting) Leinwand f
**canvass** [ˈkænvəs] vi um Stimmen
werben (for für)
**canyon** [ˈkænjən] n Felsenschlucht f;
**canyoning** [ˈkænjənɪŋ] n Canyoning nt
**cap** [kæp] n Mütze f; (lid) Verschluss m,
Deckel m
**capability** [keɪpəˈbɪlɪtɪ] n Fähigkeit f;
**capable** [ˈkeɪpəbl] adj fähig; **to be ~ of
sth** zu etw fähig (o imstande) sein; **to be
~ of doing sth** etw tun können
**capacity** [kəˈpæsɪtɪ] n (of building,
container) Fassungsvermögen nt; (ability)
Fähigkeit f; (function) **in his ~ as ...** in
seiner Eigenschaft als ...
**cape** [keɪp] n (garment) Cape nt, Umhang
m; (Geo) Kap nt
**caper** [ˈkeɪpə*] n (for cooking) Kaper f
**capital** [ˈkæpɪtl] n (Fin) Kapital nt; (letter)
Großbuchstabe m; **~ (city)** Hauptstadt f;
**capitalism** n Kapitalismus m; **capital
punishment** n die Todesstrafe
**Capricorn** [ˈkæprɪkɔːn] n (Astr) Steinbock
m
**capsize** [kæpˈsaɪz] vi kentern
**capsule** [ˈkæpsjuːl] n Kapsel f
**captain** [ˈkæptɪn] n Kapitän m; (army)
Hauptmann m
**caption** [ˈkæpʃən] n Bildunterschrift f
**captive** [ˈkæptɪv] n Gefangene(r) mf;
**capture** [ˈkæptʃə*] vt (person) fassen,
gefangen nehmen; (town etc) einnehmen;
(Inform: data) erfassen ▷ n
Gefangennahme f; (Inform) Erfassung f
**car** [kɑː*] n Auto nt; (US Rail) Wagen m
**carafe** [kəˈræf] n Karaffe f
**carambola** [kærəmˈbəʊlə] n Sternfrucht f
**caramel** [ˈkærəmel] n Karamelle f
**caravan** [ˈkærəvæn] n Wohnwagen m;
**caravan site** n Campingplatz m für
Wohnwagen
**caraway (seed)** [ˈkærəweɪ] n Kümmel m
**carbohydrate** [kɑːbəʊˈhaɪdreɪt] n
Kohle(n)hydrat nt
**car bomb** n Autobombe f

**carbon** ['kɑːbən] n Kohlenstoff m
**car boot sale** n auf einem Parkplatz stattfindender Flohmarkt
**carburettor, carburetor** (US) ['kɑːbjʊretə*] n Vergaser m
**card** [kɑːd] n Karte f; (material) Pappe f; **cardboard** ['kɑːdbɔːd] n Pappe f; **~ (box)** Karton m; (smaller) Pappschachtel f; **card game** n Kartenspiel nt
**cardiac** ['kɑːdɪæk] adj Herz-
**cardigan** ['kɑːdɪgən] n Strickjacke f
**card index** n Kartei f; **cardphone** ['kɑːdfəʊn] n Kartentelefon nt
**care** [keə*] n (worry) Sorge f; (carefulness) Sorgfalt f; (looking after things, people) Pflege f; **with ~** sorgfältig; (cautiously) vorsichtig; **to take ~** (watch out) vorsichtig sein; (in address) **~ of** bei; **to take ~ of** sorgen für, sich kümmern um ▷ vi **I don't ~** es ist mir egal; **to ~ about sth** Wert auf etw akk legen; **he ~s about her** sie liegt ihm am Herzen; **care for** vt (look after) sorgen für, sich kümmern um; (like) mögen
**career** [kə'rɪə*] n Karriere f, Laufbahn f; **career woman** (pl **women**) n Karrierefrau f; **careers adviser** n Berufsberater(in) m(f)
**carefree** ['keəfriː] adj sorgenfrei; **careful, carefully** adj, adv sorgfältig; (cautious, cautiously) vorsichtig; **careless, carelessly** adj, adv nachlässig; (driving etc) leichtsinnig; (remark) unvorsichtig; **carer** ['keərə*] n Betreuer(in) m(f), Pfleger(in) m(f); **caretaker** ['keəteɪkə*] n Hausmeister(in) m(f); **careworker** n Pfleger(in) m(f)
**car-ferry** ['kɑːferɪ] n Autofähre f
**cargo** ['kɑːgəʊ] (pl **-(e)s**) n Ladung f
**car hire** n, **car hire company** n Autovermietung f
**Caribbean** [kærɪ'biːən] n Karibik f ▷ adj karibisch
**caring** ['keərɪŋ] adj mitfühlend; (parent, partner) liebevoll; (looking after sb) fürsorglich
**car insurance** n Kraftfahrzeugversicherung f
**carnation** [kɑː'neɪʃən] n Nelke f
**carnival** ['kɑːnɪvəl] n Volksfest nt; (before Lent) Karneval m
**carol** ['kærəl] n Weihnachtslied nt
**carp** [kɑːp] n (fish) Karpfen m

**car park** n (Brit) Parkplatz m; (multi-storey car park) Parkhaus nt
**carpenter** ['kɑːpəntə*] n Zimmermann m; **carpet** ['kɑːpɪt] n Teppich m
**car phone** n Autotelefon nt; **carpool** n Fahrgemeinschaft f; (vehicles) Fuhrpark m ▷ vi eine Fahrgemeinschaft bilden; **car rental** n Autovermietung f
**carriage** ['kærɪdʒ] n (Brit Rail: coach) Wagen m; (compartment) Abteil nt; (horse-drawn) Kutsche f; (transport) Beförderung f; **carriageway** n (Brit: on road) Fahrbahn f
**carrier** ['kærɪə*] n (Comm) Spediteur(in) m(f); **carrier bag** n Tragetasche f
**carrot** ['kærət] n Karotte f
**carry** ['kærɪ] vt tragen; (in vehicle) befördern; (have on one) bei sich haben; **carry on** vi (continue) weitermachen; (fam: make a scene) ein Theater machen ▷ vt (continue) fortführen; **to ~ on working** weiter arbeiten; **carry out** vt (orders, plan) ausführen, durchführen
**carrycot** n Babytragetasche f
**carsick** ['kɑːsɪk] adj **he gets ~** ihm wird beim Autofahren übel
**cart** [kɑːt] n Wagen m, Karren m; (US: shopping trolley) Einkaufswagen m
**carton** ['kɑːtən] n (Papp)karton m; (of cigarettes) Stange f
**cartoon** [kɑː'tuːn] n Cartoon m o nt; (one drawing) Karikatur f; (film) (Zeichen)trickfilm m
**cartridge** ['kɑːtrɪdʒ] n (for film) Kassette f; (for gun, pen, printer) Patrone f; (for copier) Kartusche f
**carve** [kɑːv] vt, vi (wood) schnitzen; (stone) meißeln; (meat) schneiden, tranchieren; **carving** n (in wood) Schnitzerei f; (in stone) Skulptur f; (Ski) Carving nt
**car wash** n Autowaschanlage f
**case** [keɪs] n (crate) Kiste f; (box) Schachtel f; (for jewels) Schatulle f; (for spectacles) Etui nt; (Jur, matter) Fall m; **in ~** falls; **in that ~** in dem Fall; **in ~ of fire** bei Brand; **it's a ~ of ...** es handelt sich hier um ...
**cash** [kæʃ] n Bargeld nt; **in ~** bar; **~ on delivery** per Nachnahme ▷ vt (cheque) einlösen; **cash desk** n Kasse f; **cash dispenser** n Geldautomat m; **cashier** [kæ'ʃɪə*] n Kassierer(in) m(f); **cash machine** n (Brit) Geldautomat m

**cashmere** ['kæʃmɪə*] n Kaschmirwolle f
**cash payment** n Barzahlung f;
**cashpoint** n (Brit) Geldautomat m
**casing** ['keɪsɪŋ] n Gehäuse nt
**casino** [kə'siːnəʊ] (pl **-s**) n Kasino nt
**cask** [kɑːsk] n Fass nt
**casserole** ['kæsərəʊl] n Kasserole f; (food)
Schmortopf m
**cassette** [kæ'set] n Kassette f; **cassette
recorder** n Kassettenrekorder m
**cast** [kɑːst] (**cast, cast**) vt (throw) werfen;
(Theat, Cine) besetzen; (roles) verteilen ▷ n
(Theat, Cine) Besetzung f; (Med)
Gipsverband m; **cast off** vi (Naut)
losmachen
**caster** ['kɑːstə*] n **~ sugar** Streuzucker
m
**castle** ['kɑːsl] n Burg f
**castrate** [kæs'treɪt] vt kastrieren
**casual** ['kæʒjʊəl] adj (arrangement, remark)
beiläufig; (attitude, manner) (nach)lässig,
zwanglos; (dress) leger; (work, earnings)
Gelegenheits-; (look, glance) flüchtig;
**~ wear** Freizeitkleidung f; **~ sex**
Gelegenheitssex m; **casually** adv (remark,
say) beiläufig; (meet) zwanglos; (dressed)
leger
**casualty** ['kæʒjʊəltɪ] n Verletzte(r) mf;
(dead) Tote(r) mf; (department in hospital)
Notaufnahme f
**cat** [kæt] n Katze f; (male) Kater m
**catalog** (US), **catalogue** ['kætəlɒg] n
Katalog m ▷ vt katalogisieren
**cataract** ['kætərækt] n Wasserfall m;
(Med) grauer Star
**catarrh** [kə'tɑː*] n Katarr(h) m
**catastrophe** [kə'tæstrəfɪ] n Katastrophe
f
**catch** [kætʃ] n (fish etc) Fang m ▷ vt
(**caught, caught**) fangen; (thief) fassen;
(train, bus etc) nehmen; (not miss)
erreichen; **to ~ a cold** sich erkälten; **to
~ fire** Feuer fangen; **I didn't ~ that** das
habe ich nicht mitgekriegt; **catch on** vi
(become popular) Anklang finden; **catch up**
vt, vi **to ~ with sb** jdn einholen; **to ~ on
sth** etw nachholen; **catching** adj
ansteckend
**category** ['kætɪgərɪ] n Kategorie f
**cater** ['keɪtə*] vi die Speisen und Getränke
liefern (for für); **cater for** vt (have facilities
for) eingestellt sein auf +akk; **catering** n
Versorgung f mit Speisen und Getränken,

Gastronomie f; **catering service** n
Partyservice m
**caterpillar** ['kætəpɪlə*] n Raupe f
**cathedral** [kə'θiːdrəl] n Kathedrale f,
Dom m
**Catholic** ['kæθəlɪk] adj katholisch
▷ Katholik(in) m(f)
**cat nap** n (Brit) kurzer Schlaf; **cat's eyes**
['kætsaɪz] npl (in road) Katzenaugen pl,
Reflektoren pl
**catsup** ['kætsəp] n (US) Ketchup nt o m
**cattle** ['kætl] npl Vieh nt
**caught** [kɔːt] pt, pp of **catch**
**cauliflower** ['kɒlɪflaʊə*] n Blumenkohl m;
**cauliflower cheese** n Blumenkohl m in
Käsesoße
**cause** [kɔːz] n (origin) Ursache f (of für);
(reason) Grund m (for zu); (purpose) Sache f;
**for a good ~** für wohltätige Zwecke; **no
~ for alarm/complaint** kein Grund zur
Aufregung/Klage ▷ vt verursachen
**causeway** ['kɔːzweɪ] n Damm m
**caution** ['kɔːʃən] n Vorsicht f; (Jur, Sport)
Verwarnung f ▷ vt (ver)warnen; **cautious**
['kɔːʃəs] adj vorsichtig
**cave** [keɪv] n Höhle f; **cave in** vi
einstürzen
**cavity** ['kævɪtɪ] n Hohlraum m; (in tooth)
Loch nt
**cayenne (pepper)** [keɪ'en] n
Cayennepfeffer m
**CCTV** abbr = **closed circuit television**
Videoüberwachungsanlage f
**CD** abbr = **Compact Disc** CD f; **CD player** n
CD-Spieler m; **CD-ROM** abbr = **Compact
Disc Read Only Memory** CD-ROM f;
**CD-RW** abbr = **Compact Disc Rewritable**
CD-RW f
**cease** [siːs] vi aufhören ▷ vt beenden; **to
~ doing sth** aufhören, etw zu tun; **cease
fire** n Waffenstillstand m
**ceiling** ['siːlɪŋ] n Decke f
**celebrate** ['selɪbreɪt] vt, vi feiern;
**celebrated** adj gefeiert; **celebration**
[selɪ'breɪʃən] n Feier f; **celebrity**
[sɪ'lebrɪtɪ] n Berühmtheit f, Star m
**celeriac** [sə'lerɪæk] n (Knollen)sellerie m
o f; **celery** ['selərɪ] n (Stangen)sellerie m
o f
**cell** [sel] n Zelle f; (US) see **cellphone**
**cellar** ['selə*] n Keller m
**cello** ['tʃeləʊ] (pl **-s**) n Cello nt
**cellphone** ['selfəʊn], **cellular phone**

['seljʊlə* 'fəʊn] n Mobiltelefon nt, Handy nt

**Celt** [kelt] n Kelte m, Keltin f; **Celtic** ['keltɪk] adj keltisch ▷ n (language) Keltisch nt

**cement** [sɪ'ment] n Zement m

**cemetery** ['semɪtrɪ] n Friedhof m

**censorship** ['sensəʃɪp] n Zensur f

**cent** [sent] n (of dollar, euro etc) Cent m

**center** n (US) see **centre**

**centiliter** (US), **centilitre** ['sentɪliːtə*] n Zentiliter m; **centimeter** (US), **centimetre** ['sentɪmiːtə*] n Zentimeter m

**central** ['sentrəl] adj zentral; **Central America** n Mittelamerika nt; **Central Europe** n Mitteleuropa nt; **central heating** n Zentralheizung f; **centralize** vt zentralisieren; **central locking** n (Auto) Zentralverriegelung f; **central reservation** n (Brit) Mittelstreifen m; **central station** n Hauptbahnhof m

**centre** ['sentə*] n Mitte f; (building, of city) Zentrum nt ▷ vt zentrieren; **centre forward** n (Sport) Mittelstürmer m

**century** ['sentjʊrɪ] n Jahrhundert nt

**ceramic** [sɪ'ræmɪk] adj keramisch

**cereal** ['sɪərɪəl] n (any grain) Getreide nt; (breakfast cereal) Frühstücksflocken pl

**ceremony** ['serɪmənɪ] n Feier f, Zeremonie f

**certain** ['sɜːtən] adj sicher (of +gen); (particular) bestimmt; **for ~** mit Sicherheit; **certainly** adv sicher; (without doubt) bestimmt; **~!** aber sicher!; **~ not** ganz bestimmt nicht!

**certificate** [sə'tɪfɪkɪt] n Bescheinigung f; (in school, of qualification) Zeugnis nt; **certify** ['sɜːtɪfaɪ] vt, vi bescheinigen

**cervical smear** ['sɜːvɪkəl smɪə*] n Abstrich m

**CFC** abbr = **chlorofluorocarbon** FCKW nt

**chain** [tʃeɪn] n Kette f ▷ vt **to ~ (up)** anketten; **chain reaction** n Kettenreaktion f; **chain store** n Kettenladen m

**chair** [tʃeə*] n Stuhl m; (university) Lehrstuhl m; (armchair) Sessel m; (chairperson) Vorsitzende(r) mf; **chairlift** n Sessellift m; **chairman** (pl **-men**) n Vorsitzende(r) m; (of firm) Präsident m; **chairperson** n Vorsitzende(r) mf; (of firm) Präsident(in) m(f); **chairwoman** (pl

**-women**) n Vorsitzende f; (of firm) Präsidentin f

**chalet** ['ʃæleɪ] n (in mountains) Berghütte f; (holiday dwelling) Ferienhäuschen nt

**chalk** [tʃɔːk] n Kreide f

**challenge** ['tʃælɪndʒ] n Herausforderung f ▷ vt (person) herausfordern; (statement) bestreiten

**chambermaid** ['tʃeɪmbə*meɪd] n Zimmermädchen nt

**chamois leather** ['ʃæmwɑː'leðə*] n (for windows) Fensterleder nt

**champagne** [ʃæm'peɪn] n Champagner m

**champion** ['tʃæmpɪən] n (Sport) Meister(in) m(f); **championship** n Meisterschaft f; **Champions League** n Champions League f

**chance** [tʃɑːns] n (fate) Zufall m; (possibility) Möglichkeit f; (opportunity) Gelegenheit f; (risk) Risiko nt; **by ~** zufällig; **he doesn't stand a ~ (of winning)** er hat keinerlei Chance(, zu gewinnen)

**chancellor** ['tʃɑːnsələ*] n Kanzler(in) m(f)

**chandelier** [ʃændɪ'lɪə*] n Kronleuchter m

**change** [tʃeɪndʒ] vt verändern; (alter) ändern; (money, wheel, nappy) wechseln; (exchange) (um)tauschen; **to ~ one's clothes** sich umziehen; **to ~ trains** umsteigen; **to ~ gear** (Auto) schalten ▷ vi sich ändern; (esp outwardly) sich verändern; (get changed) sich umziehen ▷ n Veränderung f; (alteration) Änderung f; (money) Wechselgeld nt; (coins) Kleingeld nt; **for a ~** zur Abwechslung; **can you give me ~ for £10?** können Sie mir auf 10 Pfund herausgeben?; **change down** vi (Brit Auto) herunterschalten; **change over** vi sich umstellen (to auf +akk); **change up** vi (Brit Auto) hochschalten

**changeable** adj (weather) veränderlich, wechselhaft; **change machine** n Geldwechsler m; **changing room** n Umkleideraum m

**channel** ['tʃænl] n Kanal m; (Radio, TV) Kanal m, Sender m; **the (English) Channel** der Ärmelkanal; **the Channel Islands** die Kanalinseln; **the Channel Tunnel** der Kanaltunnel; **channel-hopping** n Zappen nt

**chaos** ['keɪɒs] n Chaos nt; **chaotic** [keɪ'ɒtɪk] adj chaotisch

**chap** [tʃæp] n (Brit fam) Bursche m, Kerl m

**chapel** ['tʃæpəl] n Kapelle f

**chapped** ['tʃæpt] adj (lips) aufgesprungen

**chapter** ['tʃæptə*] n Kapitel nt

**character** ['kærəktə*] n Charakter m, Wesen nt; (in a play, novel etc) Figur f; (Typo) Zeichen nt; **he's a real ~** er ist ein echtes Original; **characteristic** [kærəktə'rɪstɪk] n typisches Merkmal

**charcoal** ['tʃɑːkəʊl] n Holzkohle f

**charge** [tʃɑːdʒ] n (cost) Gebühr f; (Jur) Anklage f; **free of ~** gratis, kostenlos; **to be in ~ of** verantwortlich sein für ▷ vt (money) verlangen; (Jur) anklagen; (battery) laden; **charge card** n Kundenkreditkarte f

**charity** ['tʃærɪtɪ] n (institution) wohltätige Organisation f; **a collection for ~** eine Sammlung für wohltätige Zwecke; **charity shop** n Geschäft einer 'charity', in dem freiwillige Helfer gebrauchte Kleidung, Bücher etc verkaufen

**charm** [tʃɑːm] n Charme m ▷ vt bezaubern; **charming** adj reizend, charmant

**chart** [tʃɑːt] n Diagramm nt; (map) Karte f; **the ~s** pl die Charts, die Hitliste

**charter** ['tʃɑːtə*] n Urkunde f ▷ vt (Naut, Aviat) chartern; **charter flight** n Charterflug m

**chase** [tʃeɪs] vt jagen, verfolgen ▷ n Verfolgungsjagd f; (hunt) Jagd f

**chassis** ['ʃæsɪ] n (Auto) Fahrgestell nt

**chat** [tʃæt] vi plaudern; (Inform) chatten ▷ n Plauderei f; **chat up** vt anmachen, anbaggern; **chatroom** n (Inform) Chatroom m; **chat show** n Talkshow f; **chatty** adj geschwätzig

**chauffeur** ['ʃəʊfə*] n Chauffeur(in) m(f), Fahrer(in) m(f)

**cheap** [tʃiːp] adj billig; (of poor quality) minderwertig

**cheat** [tʃiːt] vt, vi betrügen; (in school, game) mogeln

**Chechen** ['tʃetʃen] adj tschetschenisch ▷ n Tschetschene m, Tschetschenin f; **Chechnya** ['tʃetʃnɪə] n Tschetschenien nt

**check** [tʃek] vt (examine) überprüfen (for auf +akk); (Tech: adjustment etc) kontrollieren; (US: tick) abhaken; (Aviat: luggage) einchecken; (US: coat) abgeben ▷ n (examination, restraint) Kontrolle f; (US: restaurant bill) Rechnung f; (pattern) Karo(muster) nt; (US) see **cheque**; **check in** vt, vi (Aviat) einchecken; (into hotel) sich

anmelden; **check out** vi sich abmelden, auschecken; **check up** vi nachprüfen; **to ~ on sb** Nachforschungen über jdn anstellen

**checkers** ['tʃekəz] nsing (US) Damespiel nt

**check-in** ['tʃekɪn] n (airport) Check-in m; (hotel) Anmeldung f; **check-in desk** n Abfertigungsschalter m; **checking account** n (US) Scheckkonto nt; **check list** n Kontrollliste f; **checkout** n (supermarket) Kasse f; **checkout time** n (hotel) Abreise(zeit) f; **checkpoint** n Kontrollpunkt m; **checkroom** n (US) Gepäckaufbewahrung f; **checkup** n (Med) (ärztliche) Untersuchung

**cheddar** ['tʃedə*] n Cheddarkäse m

**cheek** [tʃiːk] n Backe f, Wange f; (insolence) Frechheit f; **what a ~** so eine Frechheit!; **cheekbone** n Backenknochen m; **cheeky** adj frech

**cheer** [tʃɪə*] n Beifallsruf m; **~s** (when drinking) prost!; (Brit fam: thanks) danke; (Brit: goodbye) tschüs ▷ vt zujubeln +dat ▷ vi jubeln; **cheer up** vt aufmuntern ▷ vi fröhlicher werden; **~!** Kopf hoch!; **cheerful** ['tʃɪəfʊl] adj fröhlich

**cheese** [tʃiːz] n Käse m; **cheeseboard** n Käsebrett nt; (as course) (gemischte) Käseplatte; **cheesecake** n Käsekuchen m

**chef** [ʃef] n Koch m; (in charge of kitchen) Küchenchef(in) m(f)

**chemical** ['kemɪkəl] adj chemisch ▷ n Chemikalie f; **chemist** ['kemɪst] n (pharmacist) Apotheker(in) m(f); (industrial chemist) Chemiker(in) m(f); **~'s (shop)** n Apotheke f; **chemistry** n Chemie f

**cheque** [tʃek] n (Brit) Scheck m; **cheque account** n (Brit) Girokonto nt; **cheque book** n (Brit) Scheckheft nt; **cheque card** n (Brit) Scheckkarte f

**chequered** ['tʃekəd] adj kariert

**cherish** ['tʃerɪʃ] vt (look after) liebevoll sorgen für; (hope) hegen; (memory) bewahren

**cherry** ['tʃerɪ] n Kirsche f; **cherry tomato** (pl **-es**) n Kirschtomate f

**chess** [tʃes] n Schach nt; **chessboard** n Schachbrett nt

**chest** [tʃest] n Brust f; (box) Kiste f; **~ of drawers** Kommode f

**chestnut** ['tʃesnʌt] n Kastanie f

**chew** [tʃuː] vt, vi kauen; **chewing gum** n Kaugummi m

**chick** [tʃɪk] n Küken nt; **chicken** n Huhn nt; (food: roast) Hähnchen nt; (coward) Feigling m; **chicken breast** n Hühnerbrust f; **chicken Kiev** n paniertes Hähnchen, mit Knoblauchbutter gefüllt; **chickenpox** n Windpocken pl; **chickpea** n Kichererbse f

**chicory** ['tʃɪkərɪ] n Chicorée f

**chief** [tʃiːf] n (of department etc) Leiter(in) m(f); (boss) Chef(in) m(f); (of tribe) Häuptling m ▷ adj Haupt-; **chiefly** adv hauptsächlich

**child** [tʃaɪld] (pl **children**) n Kind nt; **child abuse** n Kindesmisshandlung f; **child allowance**, **child benefit** (Brit) n Kindergeld nt; **childbirth** n Geburt f, Entbindung f; **childhood** n Kindheit f; **childish** adj kindisch; **child lock** n Kindersicherung f; **childproof** adj kindersicher; **children** ['tʃɪldrən] pl of **child**; **child seat** n Kindersitz m

**Chile** ['tʃɪlɪ] n Chile nt

**chill** [tʃɪl] n Kühle f ▷ vt (wine) kühlen; **chill out** vi (fam) relaxen; **chilled** adj gekühlt

**chilli** ['tʃɪlɪ] n Pepperoni pl; (spice) Chili m; **chilli con carne** ['tʃɪlɪkɒn'kɑːnɪ] n Chili con carne nt

**chilly** ['tʃɪlɪ] adj kühl, frostig

**chimney** ['tʃɪmnɪ] n Schornstein m; **chimneysweep** n Schornsteinfeger(in) m(f)

**chimpanzee** [tʃɪmpæn'ziː] n Schimpanse m

**chin** [tʃɪn] n Kinn nt

**china** ['tʃaɪnə] n Porzellan nt

**China** ['tʃaɪnə] n China nt; **Chinese** [tʃaɪ'niːz] adj chinesisch ▷ n (person) Chinese m, Chinesin f; (language) Chinesisch nt; **Chinese leaves** npl Chinakohl m

**chip** [tʃɪp] n (of wood etc) Splitter m; (damage) angeschlagene Stelle; (Inform) Chip m; ~**s** (Brit: potatoes) Pommes frites pl; (US: crisps) Kartoffelchips pl ▷ vt anschlagen, beschädigen; **chippie** (fam), **chip shop** n Frittenbude f

**chiropodist** [kɪ'rɒpədɪst] n Fußpfleger(in) m(f)

**chirp** [tʃɜːp] vi zwitschern

**chisel** ['tʃɪzl] n Meißel m

**chitchat** ['tʃɪttʃæt] n Gerede nt

**chives** [tʃaɪvz] npl Schnittlauch m

**chlorine** ['klɔːriːn] n Chlor nt

**chocaholic, chocoholic** [tʃɒkə'hɒlɪk] n Schokoladenfreak m; **choc-ice** ['tʃɒkaɪs] n Eis nt mit Schokoladenüberzug; **chocolate** ['tʃɒklɪt] n Schokolade f; (chocolate-coated sweet) Praline f; **a bar of ~** eine Tafel Schokolade; **a box of ~s** eine Schachtel Pralinen; **chocolate cake** n Schokoladenkuchen m; **chocolate sauce** n Schokoladensoße f

**choice** [tʃɔɪs] n Wahl f; (selection) Auswahl f ▷ adj auserlesen; (product) Qualitäts-

**choir** ['kwaɪə*] n Chor m

**choke** [tʃəʊk] vi sich verschlucken; (Sport) die Nerven verlieren ▷ vt erdrosseln ▷ n (Auto) Choke m

**cholera** ['kɒlərə] n Cholera f

**cholesterol** [kə'lestərəl] n Cholesterin nt

**choose** [tʃuːz] (chose, chosen) vt wählen; (pick out) sich aussuchen; **there are three to ~ from** es stehen drei zur Auswahl

**chop** [tʃɒp] vt (zer)hacken; (meat etc) klein schneiden ▷ n (meat) Kotelett nt; **to get the ~** gefeuert werden; **chopper** n Hackbeil nt; (fam: helicopter) Hubschrauber m; **chopsticks** npl Essstäbchen pl

**chorus** ['kɔːrəs] n Chor m; (in song) Refrain m

**chose, chosen** [tʃəʊz, 'tʃəʊzn] pt, pp of **choose**

**chowder** ['tʃaʊdə*] n (US) dicke Suppe mit Meeresfrüchten

**christen** ['krɪsn] vt taufen; **christening** n Taufe f; **Christian** ['krɪstɪən] adj christlich ▷ n Christ(in) m(f); **Christian name** n (Brit) Vorname m

**Christmas** ['krɪsməs] n Weihnachten pl; **Christmas card** n Weihnachtskarte f; **Christmas carol** n Weihnachtslied nt; **Christmas Day** n der erste Weihnachtstag; **Christmas Eve** n Heiligabend m; **Christmas pudding** n Plumpudding m; **Christmas tree** n Weihnachtsbaum m

**chronic** ['krɒnɪk] adj (Med, fig) chronisch; (fam: very bad) miserabel

**chrysanthemum** [krɪ'sænθɪməm] n Chrysantheme f

**chubby** ['tʃʌbɪ] adj (child) pummelig; (adult) rundlich

**chuck** [tʃʌk] vt (fam) schmeißen; **chuck in** vt (fam: job) hinschmeißen; **chuck out** vt (fam) rausschmeißen; **chuck up** vi (fam) kotzen

**chunk** [tʃʌŋk] n Klumpen m; (of bread) Brocken m; (of meat) Batzen m; **chunky** adj (person) stämmig

**Chunnel** ['tʃʌnəl] n (fam) Kanaltunnel m

**church** [tʃɜːtʃ] n Kirche f; **churchyard** n Kirchhof m

**chute** [ʃuːt] n Rutsche f

**chutney** ['tʃʌtnɪ] n Chutney m

**CIA** abbr = **Central Intelligence Agency** (US) CIA f

**CID** abbr = **Criminal Investigation Department** (Brit) ≈ Kripo f

**cider** ['saɪdə*] n ≈ Apfelmost m

**cigar** [sɪ'gɑː*] n Zigarre f; **cigarette** [sɪgə'ret] n Zigarette f

**cinema** ['sɪnəmə] n Kino nt

**cinnamon** ['sɪnəmən] n Zimt m

**circa** ['sɜːkə] prep zirka

**circle** ['sɜːkl] n Kreis m ▷ vi kreisen; **circuit** ['sɜːkɪt] n Rundfahrt f; (on foot) Rundgang m; (for racing) Rennstrecke f; (Elec) Stromkreis m; **circular** ['sɜːkjʊlə*] adj (kreis)rund, kreisförmig ▷ n Rundschreiben nt; **circulation** [sɜːkjʊ'leɪʃən] n (of blood) Kreislauf m; (of newspaper) Auflage f

**circumstances** ['sɜːkəmstənsəz] npl (facts) Umstände pl; (financial condition) Verhältnisse pl; **in/under the ~** unter den Umständen; **under no ~** auf keinen Fall

**circus** ['sɜːkəs] n Zirkus m

**cissy** ['sɪsɪ] n (fam) Weichling m

**cistern** ['sɪstən] n Zisterne f; (of WC) Spülkasten m

**cite** [saɪt] vt zitieren

**citizen** ['sɪtɪzn] n Bürger(in) m(f); (of nation) Staatsangehörige(r) mf; **citizenship** n Staatsangehörigkeit f

**city** ['sɪtɪ] n Stadt f; (large) Großstadt f; **the ~** (London's financial centre) die (Londoner) City; **city centre** n Innenstadt f, Zentrum nt

**civil** ['sɪvɪl] adj (of town) Bürger-; (of state) staatsbürgerlich; (not military) zivil; **civil ceremony** n standesamtliche Hochzeit; **civil engineering** n Hoch- und Tiefbau m, Bauingenieurwesen nt; **civilian** [sɪ'vɪljən] n Zivilist(in) m(f); **civilization** [sɪvɪlaɪ'zeɪʃən] n Zivilisation f, Kultur f;

**civilized** ['sɪvɪlaɪzd] adj zivilisiert, kultiviert; **civil partnership** n eingetragene Partnerschaft; **civil rights** npl Bürgerrechte pl; **civil servant** n (Staats)beamte(r) m, (Staats)beamtin f; **civil service** n Staatsdienst m; **civil war** n Bürgerkrieg m

**CJD** abbr = **Creutzfeld-Jakob disease** Creutzfeld-Jakob-Krankheit f

**cl** abbr = **centilitre(s)** cl

**claim** [kleɪm] vt beanspruchen; (apply for) beantragen; (demand) fordern; (assert) behaupten (that dass) ▷ n (demand) Forderung f (for für); (right) Anspruch m (to auf +akk); **~ for damages** Schadensersatzforderung f; **to make** o **put in a ~** (insurance) Ansprüche geltend machen; **claimant** n Antragsteller(in) m(f)

**clam** [klæm] n Venusmuschel f; **clam chowder** n (US) dicke Muschelsuppe (mit Sellerie, Zwiebeln etc)

**clap** [klæp] vi (Beifall) klatschen

**claret** ['klærɪt] n roter Bordeaux(wein)

**clarify** ['klærɪfaɪ] vt klären

**clarinet** [klærɪ'net] n Klarinette f

**clarity** ['klærɪtɪ] n Klarheit f

**clash** [klæʃ] vi (physically) zusammenstoßen (with mit); (argue) sich auseinandersetzen (with mit); (fig: colours) sich beißen ▷ n Zusammenstoß m; (argument) Auseinandersetzung f

**clasp** [klɑːsp] n (on belt) Schnalle f

**class** [klɑːs] n Klasse f ▷ vt einordnen, einstufen

**classic** ['klæsɪk] adj (mistake, example etc) klassisch ▷ n Klassiker m; **classical** ['klæsɪkəl] adj (music, ballet etc) klassisch

**classification** [klæsɪfɪ'keɪʃn] n Klassifizierung f; **classify** ['klæsɪfaɪ] vt klassifizieren; **classified advertisement** n Kleinanzeige f

**classroom** ['klɑːsrʊm] n Klassenzimmer nt

**classy** ['klɑːsɪ] adj (fam) nobel, exklusiv

**clatter** ['klætə*] vi klappern

**clause** [klɔːz] n (Ling) Satz m; (Jur) Klausel f

**claw** [klɔː] n Kralle f

**clay** [kleɪ] n Lehm m; (for pottery) Ton m

**clean** [kliːn] adj sauber; **~ driving licence** Führerschein ohne Strafpunkte ▷ adv (completely) glatt ▷ vt sauber machen;

(carpet etc) reinigen; (window, shoes, vegetables) putzen; (wound) säubern; **clean up** vt sauber machen ▷ vi aufräumen; **cleaner** n (person) Putzmann m, Putzfrau f; (substance) Putzmittel nt; **~'s** (firm) Reinigung f

**cleanse** [klenz] vt reinigen; (wound) säubern; **cleanser** n Reinigungsmittel nt

**clear** ['klɪə*] adj klar; (distinct) deutlich; (conscience) rein; (free, road etc) frei; **to be ~ about sth** sich über etw im Klaren sein ▷ adv **to stand ~** zurücktreten ▷ vt (road, room etc) räumen; (table) abräumen; (Jur: find innocent) freisprechen (of von) ▷ vi (fog, mist) sich verziehen; (weather) aufklaren; **clear away** vt wegräumen; (dishes) abräumen; **clear off** vi (fam) abhauen; **clear up** vi (tidy up) aufräumen; (weather) sich aufklären ▷ vt (room) aufräumen; (litter) wegräumen; (matter) klären

**clearance sale** n Räumungsverkauf m; **clearing** n Lichtung f; **clearly** adv klar; (speak, remember) deutlich; (obviously) eindeutig; **clearout** n Entrümpelungsaktion f; **clearway** n (Brit) Straße f mit Halteverbot nt

**clench** [klentʃ] vt (fist) ballen; (teeth) zusammenbeißen

**clergyman** ['klɜːdʒɪmæn] (pl **-men**) n Geistliche(r) m

**clerk** [klɑːk], (US) [klɜːk] n (in office) Büroangestellte(r) mf; (US: salesperson) Verkäufer(in) m(f)

**clever** ['klevə*] adj schlau, klug; (idea) clever

**cliché** ['kliːʃeɪ] n Klischee nt

**click** [klɪk] n Klicken nt; (Inform) Mausklick m ▷ vi klicken; **to ~ on sth** (Inform) etw anklicken; **it ~ed** (fam) ich hab's/er hat's etc geschnallt, es hat gefunkt, es hat Klick gemacht; **they ~ed** sie haben sich gleich verstanden; **click on** vt (Inform) anklicken

**client** ['klaɪənt] n Kunde m, Kundin f; (Jur) Mandant(in) m(f)

**cliff** [klɪf] n Klippe f

**climate** ['klaɪmɪt] n Klima nt

**climax** ['klaɪmæks] n Höhepunkt m

**climb** [klaɪm] vi (person) klettern; (aircraft, sun) steigen; (road) ansteigen ▷ vt (mountain) besteigen; (tree etc) klettern auf +akk ▷ n Aufstieg m; **climber** n (mountaineer) Bergsteiger(in) m(f);

**climbing** n Klettern nt, Bergsteigen nt; **climbing frame** n Klettergerüst nt

**cling** [klɪŋ] (**clung, clung**) vi sich klammern (to an +akk); **cling film®** n Frischhaltefolie f

**clinic** ['klɪnɪk] n Klinik f; **clinical** adj klinisch

**clip** [klɪp] n Klammer f ▷ vt (fix) anklemmen (to an +akk); (fingernails) schneiden; **clipboard** n Klemmbrett nt; **clippers** npl Schere f; (for nails) Zwicker m

**cloak** [kləʊk] n Umhang m; **cloakroom** n (for coats) Garderobe f

**clock** [klɒk] n Uhr f; (Auto: fam) Tacho m; **round the ~** rund um die Uhr; **clockwise** adv im Uhrzeigersinn; **clockwork** n Uhrwerk nt

**clog** [klɒg] n Holzschuh m ▷ vt verstopfen

**cloister** ['klɔɪstə*] n Kreuzgang m

**clone** [kləʊn] n Klon m ▷ vt klonen

**close** [kləʊs] adj nahe (to +dat); (friend, contact) eng; (resemblance) groß; **~ to the beach** in der Nähe des Strandes; **~ win** knapper Sieg; **on ~r examination** bei näherer o genauerer Untersuchung ▷ adv [kləʊs] dicht; **he lives ~ by** er wohnt ganz in der Nähe ▷ vt [kləʊz] schließen; (road) sperren; (discussion, matter) abschließen ▷ vi [kləʊz] schließen ▷ n [kləʊz] Ende nt; **close down** vi schließen; (factory) stillgelegt werden ▷ vt (shop) schließen; (factory) stilllegen; **closed** adj (road) gesperrt; (shop etc) geschlossen; **closed circuit television** n Videoüberwachungsanlage f; **closely** adv (related) eng, nah; (packed, follow) dicht; (attentively) genau

**closet** ['klɒzɪt] n (esp US) Schrank m

**close-up** ['kləʊsʌp] n Nahaufnahme f

**closing** ['kləʊzɪŋ] adj **~ date** letzter Termin; (for competition) Einsendeschluss m; **~ time** (of shop) Ladenschluss m; (Brit: of pub) Polizeistunde f

**clot** [klɒt] n (blood) **~** Blutgerinnsel nt; (fam: idiot) Trottel m ▷ vi (blood) gerinnen

**cloth** [klɒθ] n (material) Tuch nt; (for cleaning) Lappen m

**clothe** [kləʊð] vt kleiden; **clothes** npl Kleider pl, Kleidung f; **clothes line** n Wäscheleine f; **clothes peg, clothespin** (US) n Wäscheklammer f; **clothing** ['kləʊðɪŋ] n Kleidung f

**clotted** ['klɒtɪd] adj ~ **cream** dicke Sahne (aus erhitzter Milch)

**cloud** [klaʊd] n Wolke f; **cloudy** adj (sky) bewölkt; (liquid) trüb

**clove** [kləʊv] n Gewürznelke f; ~ **of garlic** Knoblauchzehe f

**clover** ['kləʊvə*] n Klee m; **cloverleaf** (pl -leaves) n Kleeblatt nt

**clown** [klaʊn] n Clown m

**club** [klʌb] n (weapon) Knüppel m; (society) Klub m, Verein m; (nightclub) Disko f; (golf club) Golfschläger m; ~**s** (Cards) Kreuz nt; **clubbing** n **to go** ~ in die Disko gehen; **club class** n (Aviat) Businessclass f

**clue** [kluː] n Anhaltspunkt m, Hinweis m; **he hasn't a** ~ er hat keine Ahnung

**clumsy** ['klʌmzɪ] adj unbeholfen, ungeschickt

**clung** [klʌŋ] pt, pp of **cling**

**clutch** [klʌtʃ] n (Auto) Kupplung f ▷ vt umklammern; (book etc) an sich akk klammern

**cm** abbr = **centimetre(s)** cm

**c/o** abbr = **care of** bei

**Co** abbr = **company** Co

**coach** [kəʊtʃ] n (Brit: bus) Reisebus m; (Rail) (Personen)wagen m; (Sport: trainer) Trainer(in) m(f) ▷ vt Nachhilfeunterricht geben +dat; (Sport) trainieren; **coach (class)** n (Aviat) Economyclass f; **coach driver** n Busfahrer(in) m(f); **coach station** n Busbahnhof m; **coach trip** n Busfahrt f; (tour) Busreise f

**coal** [kəʊl] n Kohle f

**coalition** [kəʊə'lɪʃən] n (Pol) Koalition f

**coalmine** ['kəʊlmaɪn] n Kohlenbergwerk nt; **coalminer** n Bergarbeiter m

**coast** [kəʊst] n Küste f; **coastguard** n Küstenwache f; **coastline** n Küste f

**coat** [kəʊt] n Mantel m; (jacket) Jacke f; (on animals) Fell nt, Pelz m; (of paint) Schicht f; ~ **of arms** Wappen nt; **coathanger** n Kleiderbügel m; **coating** n Überzug m; (layer) Schicht f

**cobble(stone)s** ['kɒbl(stəʊn)z] npl Kopfsteine pl; (surface) Kopfsteinpflaster nt

**cobweb** ['kɒbweb] n Spinnennetz nt

**cocaine** [kə'keɪn] n Kokain nt

**cock** [kɒk] n Hahn m; (vulg: penis) Schwanz m; **cockerel** ['kɒkərəl] n junger Hahn

**cockle** ['kɒkl] n Herzmuschel f

**cockpit** ['kɒkpɪt] n (in plane, racing car) Cockpit nt; **cockroach** ['kɒkrəʊtʃ] n Kakerlake f; **cocksure** adj todsicher; **cocktail** ['kɒkteɪl] n Cocktail m; **cock-up** n (Brit fam) **to make a** ~ **of sth** bei etw Mist bauen; **cocky** ['kɒkɪ] adj großspurig, von sich selbst überzeugt

**cocoa** ['kəʊkəʊ] n Kakao m

**coconut** ['kəʊkənʌt] n Kokosnuss f

**cod** [kɒd] n Kabeljau m

**COD** abbr = **cash on delivery** per Nachnahme

**code** [kəʊd] n Kode m

**coeducational** [kəʊedjʊ'keɪʃənl] adj (school) gemischt

**coffee** ['kɒfɪ] n Kaffee m; **coffee bar** n Café nt; **coffee break** n Kaffeepause f; **coffee maker** n Kaffeemaschine f; **coffee pot** n Kaffeekanne f; **coffee shop** n Café nt; **coffee table** n Couchtisch m

**coffin** ['kɒfɪn] n Sarg m

**coil** [kɔɪl] n Rolle f; (Elec) Spule f; (Med) Spirale f

**coin** [kɔɪn] n Münze f

**coincide** [kəʊɪn'saɪd] vi (happen together) zusammenfallen (with mit); **coincidence** [kəʊ'ɪnsɪdəns] n Zufall m

**coke** [kəʊk] n Koks m; **Coke®** Cola f

**cola** ['kəʊlə] n Cola f

**cold** [kəʊld] adj kalt; **I'm** ~ mir ist kalt, ich friere ▷ n Kälte f; (illness) Erkältung f, Schnupfen m; **to catch a** ~ sich erkälten; **cold box** n Kühlbox f; **coldness** n Kälte f; **cold sore** n Herpes m; **cold turkey** n (fam) Totalentzug m; (symptoms) Entzugserscheinungen pl

**coleslaw** ['kəʊlslɔː] n Krautsalat m

**collaborate** [kə'læbəreɪt] vi zusammenarbeiten (with mit); **collaboration** [kəlæbə'reɪʃən] n Zusammenarbeit f; (of one party) Mitarbeit f

**collapse** [kə'læps] vi zusammenbrechen; (building etc) einstürzen ▷ n Zusammenbruch m; (of building) Einsturz m; **collapsible** [kə'læpsəbl] adj zusammenklappbar, Klapp-

**collar** ['kɒlə*] n Kragen m; (for dog, cat) Halsband nt; **collarbone** n Schlüsselbein nt

**colleague** ['kɒliːg] n Kollege m, Kollegin f

**collect** [kə'lekt] vt sammeln; (fetch) abholen ▷ vi sich sammeln; **collect call** n

(US) R-Gespräch nt; **collected** adj (works) gesammelt; (person) gefasst; **collector** n Sammler(in) m(f); **collection** [kə'lekʃən] n Sammlung f; (Rel) Kollekte f; (from postbox) Leerung f

**college** ['kɒlɪdʒ] n (residential) College nt; (specialist) Fachhochschule f; (vocational) Berufsschule f; (US: university) Universität f; **to go to ~** (US) studieren

**collide** [kə'laɪd] vi zusammenstoßen; **collision** [kə'lɪʒən] n Zusammenstoß m

**colloquial** [kə'ləʊkwɪəl] adj umgangssprachlich

**Cologne** [kə'ləʊn] n Köln nt

**colon** ['kəʊlən] n (punctuation mark) Doppelpunkt m

**colonial** [kə'ləʊnɪəl] adj Kolonial-; **colonize** ['kɒlənaɪz] vt kolonisieren; **colony** ['kɒlənɪ] n Kolonie f

**color** n (US), **colour** ['kʌlə*] n Farbe f; (of skin) Hautfarbe f ▷ vt anmalen; (bias) färben; **colour-blind** adj farbenblind; **coloured** adj farbig; (biased) gefärbt; **colour film** n Farbfilm m; **colourful** adj (lit, fig) bunt; (life, past) bewegt; **colouring** n (in food etc) Farbstoff m; (complexion) Gesichtsfarbe f; **colourless** adj (lit, fig) farblos; **colour photo(graph)** n Farbfoto nt; **colour television** n Farbfernsehen nt

**column** ['kɒləm] n Säule f; (of print) Spalte f

**comb** [kəʊm] n Kamm m ▷ vt kämmen; **to ~ one's hair** sich kämmen

**combination** [kɒmbɪ'neɪʃən] n Kombination f; (mixture) Mischung f (of aus); **combine** [kəm'baɪn] vt verbinden; (with mit); (two things) kombinieren

**come** [kʌm] (**came, come**) vi kommen; (arrive) ankommen; (on list, in order) stehen; (with adjective: become) werden; **~ and see us** besuchen Sie uns mal; **coming** ich komm ja schon!; **to ~ first/second** erster/zweiter werden; **to ~ true** wahr werden; **to ~ loose** sich lockern; **the years to ~** die kommenden Jahre; **there's one more to ~** es kommt noch eins/noch einer; **how ~ ...?** (fam) wie kommt es, dass ...?; **~ to think of it** (fam) wo es mir gerade einfällt; **come across** vt (find) stoßen auf +akk; **come back** vi zurückkommen; **I'll ~ to that** ich komme darauf zurück; **come down** vi herunterkommen; (rain, snow, price) fallen;

**come from** vt (result) kommen von; **where do you ~?** wo kommen Sie her?; **I ~ London** ich komme aus London; **come in** vi hereinkommen; (arrive) ankommen; (in race) **to ~ fourth** Vierter werden; **come off** vi (button, handle etc) abgehen; (succeed) gelingen; **to ~ well/badly** gut/schlecht wegkommen; **come on** vi (progress) vorankommen; **~! komm!**; (hurry) beeil dich!; (encouraging) los!; **come out** vi herauskommen; (photo) was werden; (homosexual) sich outen; **come round** vi (visit) vorbeikommen; (regain consciousness) wieder zu sich kommen; **come to** vi (regain consciousness) wieder zu sich kommen ▷ vt (sum) sich belaufen auf +akk; **when it comes to ...** wenn es um ... geht; **come up** vi hochkommen; (sun, moon) aufgehen; **to ~ (for discussion)** zur Sprache kommen; **come up to** vt (approach) zukommen auf +akk; (water) reichen bis zu; (expectations) entsprechen +dat; **come up with** vt (idea) haben; (solution, answer) kommen auf +akk; **to ~ a suggestion** einen Vorschlag machen

**comedian** [kə'miːdɪən] n Komiker(in) m(f)

**comedown** ['kʌmdaʊn] n Abstieg m

**comedy** ['kɒmədɪ] n Komödie f

**come-on** ['kʌmɒn] n **to give sb the ~** (fam) jdn anmachen

**comfort** ['kʌmfət] n Komfort m; (consolation) Trost m ▷ vt trösten; **comfortable** adj bequem; (income) ausreichend; (temperature, life) angenehm; **comfort station** n (US) Toilette f; **comforting** adj tröstlich

**comic** ['kɒmɪk] n (magazine) Comic(heft) nt; (comedian) Komiker(in) m(f) ▷ adj komisch

**coming** ['kʌmɪŋ] adj kommend; (event) bevorstehend

**comma** ['kɒmə] n Komma nt

**command** [kə'mɑːnd] n Befehl m; (control) Führung f; (Mil) Kommando nt ▷ vt befehlen +dat

**commemorate** [kə'meməreɪt] vt gedenken +gen; **commemoration** [kəmemə'reɪʃən] n **in ~ of** in Gedenken an +akk

**comment** ['kɒment] n (remark) Bemerkung f; (note) Anmerkung f; (official) Kommentar m (on zu); **no ~** kein

Kommentar ⊳ *vi* sich äußern (*on* zu);
**commentary** ['kɒməntrı] *n* Kommentar
*m* (*on* zu); (*Tv, Sport*) Livereportage *f*;
**commentator** ['kɒmənteɪtə*] *n*
Kommentator(in) *m(f)*; (*Tv, Sport*)
Reporter(in) *m(f)*
**commerce** ['kɒmɜːs] *n* Handel *m*;
**commercial** [kə'mɜːʃəl] *adj* kommerziell;
(*training*) kaufmännisch; **~ break**
Werbepause *f*; **~ vehicle** Lieferwagen *m*
⊳ *n* (*Tv*) Werbespot *m*
**commission** [kə'mɪʃən] *n* Auftrag *m*; (*fee*)
Provision *f*; (*reporting body*) Kommission *f*
⊳ *vt* beauftragen
**commit** [kə'mɪt] *vt* (*crime*) begehen ⊳ *vr*
**to ~ oneself** (*undertake*) sich verpflichten
(*to* zu); **commitment** *n* Verpflichtung *f*;
(*Pol*) Engagement *nt*
**committee** [kə'mɪtɪ] *n* Ausschuss *m*,
Komitee *nt*
**commodity** [kə'mɒdɪtɪ] *n* Ware *f*
**common** ['kɒmən] *adj* (*experience*)
allgemein, alltäglich; (*shared*) gemeinsam;
(*widespread, frequent*) häufig; (*pej*)
gewöhnlich, ordinär; **to have sth in ~** etw
gemein haben ⊳ *n* (*Brit: land*)
Gemeindewiese *f*; **commonly** *adv* häufig,
allgemein; **commonplace** *adj* alltäglich;
(*pej*) banal; **commonroom** *n*
Gemeinschaftsraum *m*; **Commons** *n* (*Brit
Pol*) **the (House of) ~** das Unterhaus;
**common sense** *n* gesunder
Menschenverstand; **Commonwealth** *n*
Commonwealth *nt*; **~ of Independent
States** Gemeinschaft *f* Unabhängiger
Staaten
**communal** ['kɒmjʊnl] *adj* gemeinsam;
(*of a community*) Gemeinschafts-,
Gemeinde-
**communicate** [kə'mjuːnɪkeɪt] *vi*
kommunizieren (*with* mit);
**communication** [kəmjuːnɪ'keɪʃən] *n*
Kommunikation *f*, Verständigung *f*;
**communications satellite** *n*
Nachrichtensatellit *m*;
**communications technology** *n*
Nachrichtentechnik *f*; **communicative**
*adj* gesprächig
**communion** [kə'mjuːnɪən] *n* (*Holy*)
**Communion** Heiliges Abendmahl;
(*Catholic*) Kommunion *f*
**communism** ['kɒmjʊnɪzəm] *n*
Kommunismus *m*; **communist**

['kɒmjʊnɪst] *adj* kommunistisch ⊳ *n*
Kommunist(in) *m(f)*
**community** [kə'mjuːnɪtɪ] *n*
Gemeinschaft *f*; **community centre** *n*
Gemeindezentrum *nt*; **community
service** *n* (*Jur*) Sozialdienst *m*
**commutation ticket** [kɒmjʊ'teɪʃəntɪkɪt]
*n* (*US*) Zeitkarte *f*; **commute** [kə'mjuːt] *vi*
pendeln; **commuter** *n* Pendler(in) *m(f)*
**compact** [kəm'pækt] *adj* kompakt
⊳ ['kɒmpækt] *n* (*for make-up*) Puderdose *f*;
(*US: car*) ≈ Mittelklassewagen *m*; **compact
camera** *n* Kompaktkamera *f*; **compact
disc** *n* Compact Disc *f*, CD *f*
**companion** [kəm'pænɪən] *n*
Begleiter(in) *m(f)*
**company** ['kʌmpənɪ] *n* Gesellschaft *f*;
(*Comm*) Firma *f*; **to keep sb ~** jdm
Gesellschaft leisten; **company car** *n*
Firmenauto *nt*
**comparable** ['kɒmpərəbl] *adj*
vergleichbar (*with, to* mit)
**comparative** [kəm'pærətɪv] *adj* relativ
⊳ *n* (*Ling*) Komparativ *m*; **comparatively**
*adv* verhältnismäßig
**compare** [kəm'pɛə*] *vt* vergleichen (*with,
to* mit); **~d with** *o* **to** im Vergleich zu;
**beyond ~** unvergleichlich; **comparison**
[kəm'pærɪsn] *n* Vergleich *m*; **in ~ with** im
Vergleich mit (*o* zu)
**compartment** [kəm'pɑːtmənt] *n* (*Rail*)
Abteil *nt*; (*in desk etc*) Fach *nt*
**compass** ['kʌmpəs] *n* Kompass *m*; **~es** *pl*
Zirkel *m*
**compassion** [kəm'pæʃən] *n* Mitgefühl *nt*
**compatible** [kəm'pætɪbl] *adj* vereinbar
(*with* mit); (*Inform*) kompatibel; **we're not
~** wir passen nicht zueinander
**compensate** ['kɒmpənseɪt] *vt* (*person*)
entschädigen (*for* für) ⊳ *vi* **to ~ for sth**
Ersatz für etw leisten; (*make up for*) etw
ausgleichen; **compensation**
[kɒmpən'seɪʃən] *n* Entschädigung *f*;
(*money*) Schadenersatz *m*; (*Jur*) Abfindung *f*
**compete** [kəm'piːt] *vi* konkurrieren (*for*
um); (*Sport*) kämpfen (*for* um); (*take part*)
teilnehmen (*in* an +*dat*)
**competence** ['kɒmpɪtəns] *n* Fähigkeit *f*;
(*Jur*) Zuständigkeit *f*; **competent** *adj*
fähig; (*Jur*) zuständig
**competition** [kɒmpɪ'tɪʃən] *n* (*contest*)
Wettbewerb *m*; (*Comm*) Konkurrenz *f* (*for*
um); **competitive** [kəm'petɪtɪv] *adj* (*firm,*

*price, product)* konkurrenzfähig;
**competitor** [kəm'petɪtə*] *n (Comm)*
Konkurrent(in) *m(f)*; *(Sport)* Teilnehmer(in)
*m(f)*

**complain** [kəm'pleɪn] *vi* klagen; *(formally)*
sich beschweren *(about* über +*akk)*;
**complaint** *n* Klage *f*, *(formal)* Beschwerde
*f*; *(Med)* Leiden *nt*

**complement** *vt* ergänzen

**complete** [kəm'pli:t] *adj* vollständig;
*(finished)* fertig; *(failure, disaster)* total;
*(happiness)* vollkommen; **are we ~?** sind
wir vollzählig? ▷ *vt* vervollständigen;
*(finish)* beenden; *(form)* ausfüllen;
**completely** *adv* völlig; **not ~ ...** nicht
ganz ...

**complex** ['kɒmpleks] *adj* komplex; *(task,
theory etc)* kompliziert ▷ *n* Komplex *m*

**complexion** [kəm'plekʃən] *n*
Gesichtsfarbe *f*, Teint *m*

**complicated** ['kɒmplɪkeɪtɪd] *adj*
kompliziert; **complication**
['kɒmplɪkeɪʃən] *n* Komplikation *f*

**compliment** ['kɒmplɪmənt] *n*
Kompliment *nt*; **complimentary**
[kɒmplɪ'mentərɪ] *adj* lobend; *(free of
charge)* Gratis-; **~ ticket** Freikarte *f*

**comply** [kəm'plaɪ] *vi* **to ~ with the
regulations** den Vorschriften
entsprechen

**component** [kəm'pəʊnənt] *n*
Bestandteil *m*

**compose** [kəm'pəʊz] *vt (music)*
komponieren; **to ~ oneself** sich
zusammennehmen; **composed** *adj*
gefasst; **to be ~ of** bestehen aus;
**composer** *n* Komponist(in) *m(f)*;
**composition** [kɒmpə'zɪʃən] *n (of a group)*
Zusammensetzung *f*; *(Mus)* Komposition *f*

**comprehend** [kɒmprɪ'hend] *vt*
verstehen; **comprehension**
[kɒmprɪ'henʃən] *n* Verständnis *nt*

**comprehensive** [kɒmprɪ'hensɪv] *adj*
umfassend; **~ school** Gesamtschule *f*

**compress** [kəm'pres] *vt* komprimieren

**comprise** [kəm'praɪz] *vt* umfassen,
bestehen aus

**compromise** ['kɒmprəmaɪz] *n*
Kompromiss *m* ▷ *vi* einen Kompromiss
schließen

**compulsory** [kəm'pʌlsərɪ] *adj*
obligatorisch; **~ subject** Pflichtfach *nt*

**computer** [kəm'pju:tə*] *n* Computer *m*;

**computer aided** *adj* computergestützt;
**computer-controlled** *adj*
rechnergesteuert; **computer game** *n*
Computerspiel *nt*; **computer-literate** *adj*
**to be ~** mit dem Computer umgehen
können; **computer scientist** *n*
Informatiker(in) *m(f)*; **computing** *n*
*(subject)* Informatik *f*

**con** [kɒn] *(fam)* *n* Schwindel *m* ▷ *vt*
betrügen *(out of* um*)*

**conceal** [kən'si:l] *vt* verbergen *(from* vor
+*dat)*

**conceivable** [kən'si:vəbl] *adj* denkbar,
vorstellbar; **conceive** [kən'si:v] *vt*
*(imagine)* sich vorstellen; *(child)*
empfangen

**concentrate** ['kɒnsəntreɪt] *vi* sich
konzentrieren *(on* auf +*akk)*;
**concentration** [kɒnsən'treɪʃən] *n*
Konzentration *f*

**concept** ['kɒnsept] *n* Begriff *m*

**concern** [kən'sɜ:n] *n (affair)*
Angelegenheit *f*, *(worry)* Sorge *f*;
*(Comm: firm)* Unternehmen *nt*; **it's not my
~** das geht mich nichts an; **there's
no cause for ~** kein Grund zur
Beunruhigung ▷ *vt (affect)* angehen;
*(have connection with)* betreffen; *(be
about)* handeln von; **those ~ed** die
Betroffenen; **as far as I'm ~ed** was
mich betrifft; **concerned** *adj (anxious)*
besorgt; **concerning** *prep* bezüglich,
hinsichtlich +*gen*

**concert** ['kɒnsət] *n* Konzert *nt*; **~ hall**
Konzertsaal *m*

**concession** [kən'seʃən] *n* Zugeständnis
*nt*; *(reduction)* Ermäßigung *f*

**concise** [kən'saɪs] *adj* knapp gefasst,
prägnant

**conclude** [kən'klu:d] *vt (end)* beenden,
*(ab)schließen; *(infer)* folgern *(from* aus*)*; **to
~ that ...** zu dem Schluss kommen, dass
...; **conclusion** [kən'klu:ʒən] *n* Schluss *m*,
Schlussfolgerung *f*

**concrete** ['kɒŋkri:t] *n* Beton *m* ▷ *adj*
konkret

**concussion** [kən'kʌʃən] *n*
Gehirnerschütterung *f*

**condemn** [kən'dem] *vt* verdammen; *(esp
Jur)* verurteilen

**condensed milk** *n* Kondensmilch *f*,
Dosenmilch *f*

**condition** [kən'dɪʃən] *n (state)* Zustand *m*;

(*requirement*) Bedingung *f*; **on ~ that ...** unter der Bedingung, dass ...; **~s** *pl* (*circumstances, weather*) Verhältnisse *pl*; **conditional** *adj* bedingt; (*Ling*) Konditional-; **conditioner** *n* Weichspüler *m*; (*for hair*) Pflegespülung *f*

**condo** ['kɒndəʊ] (*pl* **-s**) *n see* **condominium**

**condolences** [kən'dəʊlənsɪz] *npl* Beileid *nt*

**condom** ['kɒndəm] *n* Kondom *nt*

**condominium** [kɒndə'mɪnɪəm] *n* (*US: apartment*) Eigentumswohnung *f*

**conduct** *n* ['kɒndʌkt] *n* (*behaviour*) Verhalten *nt* ▷ [kən'dʌkt] *vt* führen, leiten; (*orchestra*) dirigieren; **conductor** [kən'dʌktə*] *n* (*of orchestra*) Dirigent(in) *m(f)*; (*in bus*) Schaffner(in) *m(f)*; (*US: on train*) Zugführer(in) *m(f)*

**cone** [kəʊn] *n* Kegel *m*; (*for ice cream*) Waffeltüte *f*; (*fir cone*) (Tannen)zapfen *m*

**conference** ['kɒnfərəns] *n* Konferenz *f*

**confess** [kən'fes] *vt, vi* **to ~ that ...** gestehen, dass ...; **confession** [kən'feʃən] *n* Geständnis *nt*; (*Rel*) Beichte *f*

**confetti** [kən'fetɪ] *n* Konfetti *nt*

**confidence** ['kɒnfɪdəns] *n* Vertrauen *nt* (*in zu*); (*assurance*) Selbstvertrauen *nt*; **confident** *adj* (*sure*) zuversichtlich (*that ... dass ...*), überzeugt (*of von*); (*self-assured*) selbstsicher; **confidential** [kɒnfɪ'denʃəl] *adj* vertraulich

**confine** [kən'faɪn] *vt* beschränken (*to auf +akk*)

**confirm** [kən'fɜːm] *vt* bestätigen; **confirmation** [kɒnfə'meɪʃən] *n* Bestätigung *f*; (*Rel*) Konfirmation *f*; **confirmed** *adj* überzeugt; (*bachelor*) eingefleischt

**confiscate** ['kɒnfɪskeɪt] *vt* beschlagnahmen, konfiszieren

**conflict** ['kɒnflɪkt] *n* Konflikt *m*

**confuse** [kən'fjuːz] *vt* verwirren; (*sth with sth*) verwechseln (*with mit*); (*several things*) durcheinanderbringen; **confused** *adj* (*person*) konfus, verwirrt; (*account*) verworren; **confusing** *adj* verwirrend; **confusion** [kən'fjuːʒən] *n* Verwirrung *f*; (*of two things*) Verwechslung *f*; (*muddle*) Chaos *nt*

**congested** [kən'dʒestɪd] *adj* verstopft; (*overcrowded*) überfüllt; **congestion** [kən'dʒestʃən] *n* Stau *m*

**congratulate** [kən'grætjʊleɪt] *vt* gratulieren (*on zu*); **congratulations** [kəngrætjʊ'leɪʃənz] *npl* Glückwünsche *pl*; **~!** gratuliere!, herzlichen Glückwunsch!

**congregation** [kɒngrɪ'geɪʃən] *n* (*Rel*) Gemeinde *f*

**congress** ['kɒngres] *n* Kongress *m*; (*US*) **Congress** der Kongress; **congressman** (*pl* **-men**), **congresswoman** (*pl* **-women**) *n* (*US*) Mitglied *nt* des Repräsentantenhauses

**conifer** ['kɒnɪfə*] *n* Nadelbaum *m*

**conjunction** [kən'dʒʌŋkʃən] *n* (*Ling*) Konjunktion *f*; **in ~ with** in Verbindung mit

**conk out** [kɒŋk 'aʊt] *vi* (*fam: appliance, car*) den Geist aufgeben, streiken; (*person: die*) ins Gras beißen

**connect** [kə'nekt] *vt* verbinden (*with, to mit*); (*Elec, Tech: appliance etc*) anschließen (*to an +akk*) ▷ *vi* (*train, plane*) Anschluss haben (*with an +akk*); **~ing flight** Anschlussflug *m*; **~ing train** Anschlusszug *m*; **connection** [kə'nekʃən] *n* Verbindung *f*; (*link*) Zusammenhang *m*; (*for train, plane, electrical appliance*) Anschluss *m* (*with, to an +akk*); (*business etc*) Beziehung *f*; **in ~ with** in Zusammenhang mit; **bad ~** (*Tel*) schlechte Verbindung; (*Elec*) Wackelkontakt *m*; **connector** *n* (*Inform: computer*) Stecker *m*

**conscience** ['kɒnʃəns] *n* Gewissen *nt*; **conscientious** [kɒnʃɪ'enʃəs] *adj* gewissenhaft

**conscious** ['kɒnʃəs] *adj* (*act*) bewusst; (*Med*) bei Bewusstsein; **to be ~** bei Bewusstsein sein; **consciousness** *n* Bewusstsein *nt*

**consecutive** [kən'sekjʊtɪv] *adj* aufeinander folgend

**consent** [kən'sent] *n* Zustimmung *f* ▷ *vi* zustimmen (*to dat*)

**consequence** ['kɒnsɪkwəns] *n* Folge *f*, Konsequenz *f*; **consequently** ['kɒnsɪkwəntlɪ] *adv* folglich

**conservation** [kɒnsə'veɪʃən] *n* Erhaltung *f*; (*of buildings*) Denkmalschutz *m*; (*nature conservation*) Naturschutz *m*; **conservation area** *n* Naturschutzgebiet *nt*; (*in town*) unter Denkmalschutz stehendes Gebiet

**Conservative** [kən'sɜːvətɪv] *adj* (*Pol*) konservativ

**conservatory** [kən'sɜːvətrɪ] n
(greenhouse) Gewächshaus nt; (room)
Wintergarten m

**consider** [kən'sɪdə*] vt (reflect on)
nachdenken über, sich überlegen; (take
into account) in Betracht ziehen; (regard)
halten für; **he is ~ed (to be)** ... er gilt als
...; **considerable** [kən'sɪdərəbl] adj
beträchtlich; **considerate** [kən'sɪdərɪt]
adj aufmerksam, rücksichtsvoll;
**consideration** [kənsɪdə'reɪʃən] n
(thoughtfulness) Rücksicht f; (thought)
Überlegung f; **to take sth into ~** etw in
Betracht ziehen; **considering**
[kən'sɪdərɪŋ] prep in Anbetracht +gen
▷ conj da

**consist** [kən'sɪst] vi **to ~ of** ... bestehen
aus ...

**consistent** [kən'sɪstənt] adj (behaviour,
process etc) konsequent; (statements)
übereinstimmend; (argument) folgerichtig;
(performance, results) beständig

**consolation** [kɒnsə'leɪʃən] n Trost m;
**console** [kən'səʊl] vt trösten

**consolidate** [kən'sɒlɪdeɪt] vt festigen

**consonant** ['kɒnsənənt] n Konsonant m

**conspicuous** [kən'spɪkjʊəs] adj auffällig,
auffallend

**conspiracy** [kən'spɪrəsɪ] n Komplott nt;
**conspire** [kən'spaɪə*] vi sich
verschwören (against gegen)

**constable** ['kʌnstəbl] n (Brit) Polizist(in)
m(f)

**Constance** ['kɒnstəns] n Konstanz nt;
**Lake ~** der Bodensee

**constant** ['kɒnstənt] adj (continual)
ständig, dauernd; (unchanging: temperature
etc) gleich bleibend; **constantly** adv
dauernd

**consternation** [kɒnstə'neɪʃən] n
(dismay) Bestürzung f

**constituency** [kən'stɪtjʊənsɪ] n
Wahlkreis m

**constitution** [kɒnstɪ'tjuːʃən] n
Verfassung f; (of person) Konstitution f

**construct** [kən'strʌkt] vt bauen;
**construction** [kən'strʌkʃən] n (process,
result) Bau m; (method) Bauweise f; **under
~** im Bau befindlich; **construction site** n
Baustelle f; **construction worker** n
Bauarbeiter(in) m(f)

**consulate** ['kɒnsjʊlət] n Konsulat nt

**consult** [kən'sʌlt] vt um Rat fragen;

(doctor) konsultieren; (book) nachschlagen
in +dat; **consultant** n (Med) Facharzt m,
Fachärztin f; **consultation** [kɒnsəl'teɪʃən]
n Beratung f; (Med) Konsultation f

**consume** [kən'sjuːm] vt verbrauchen;
(food) konsumieren; **consumer** n
Verbraucher(in) m(f); **consumer-friendly**
adj verbraucherfreundlich

**contact** ['kɒntækt] n (touch) Berührung f;
(communication) Kontakt m; (person)
Kontaktperson f; **to be/keep in ~ (with
sb)** (mit jdm) in Kontakt sein/bleiben ▷ vt
sich in Verbindung setzen mit; **contact
lenses** npl Kontaktlinsen pl

**contagious** [kən'teɪdʒəs] adj ansteckend

**contain** [kən'teɪn] vt enthalten;
**container** n Behälter m; (for transport)
Container m

**contaminate** [kən'tæmɪneɪt] vt
verunreinigen; (chemically) verseuchen; **~d
by radiation** strahlenverseucht,
verstrahlt; **contamination**
[kəntæmɪ'neɪʃən] n Verunreinigung f; (by
radiation) Verseuchung f

**contemporary** [kən'tempərərɪ] adj
zeitgenössisch

**contempt** [kən'tempt] n Verachtung f;
**contemptuous** adj verächtlich; **to be
~** voller Verachtung sein (of für)

**content** [kən'tent] adj zufrieden

**content(s)** ['kɒntent(s)] n pl Inhalt m

**contest** ['kɒntest] n (Wett)kampf m (for
um); (competition) Wettbewerb m
▷ [kən'test] vt kämpfen um +akk; (dispute)
bestreiten; **contestant** [kən'testənt] n
Teilnehmer(in) m(f)

**context** ['kɒntekst] n Zusammenhang m;
**out of ~** aus dem Zusammenhang
gerissen

**continent** ['kɒntɪnənt] n Kontinent m,
Festland nt; **the Continent** (Brit) das
europäische Festland, der Kontinent;
**continental** [kɒntɪ'nentl] adj
kontinental; **~ breakfast** kleines
Frühstück mit Brötchen und Marmelade, Kaffee
oder Tee

**continual** [kən'tɪnjʊəl] adj (endless)
ununterbrochen; (constant) dauernd,
ständig; **continually** adv dauernd; (again
and again) immer wieder; **continuation**
[kəntɪnjʊ'eɪʃən] n Fortsetzung f;
**continue** [kən'tɪnjuː] vi weitermachen
(with mit); (esp talking) fortfahren (with

mit); (*travelling*) weiterfahren; (*state, conditions*) fortdauern, anhalten ▷ *vt* fortsetzen; **to be ~d** Fortsetzung folgt; **continuous** [kən'tɪnjʊəs] *adj* (*endless*) ununterbrochen; (*constant*) ständig

**contraceptive** [kɒntrə'sɛptɪv] *n* Verhütungsmittel *nt*

**contract** ['kɒntrækt] *n* Vertrag *m*

**contradict** [kɒntrə'dɪkt] *vt* widersprechen +*dat*; **contradiction** [kɒntrə'dɪkʃən] *n* Widerspruch *m*

**contrary** ['kɒntrərɪ] *n* Gegenteil *nt*; **on the ~** im Gegenteil ▷ *adj* **~ to** entgegen +*dat*

**contrast** ['kɒntrɑːst] *n* Kontrast *m*, Gegensatz *m*; **in ~ to** im Gegensatz zu ▷ [kən'trɑːst] *vt* entgegensetzen

**contribute** [kən'trɪbjuːt] *vt, vi* beitragen (*to* zu); (*money*) spenden (*to* für); **contribution** [kɒntrɪ'bjuːʃən] *n* Beitrag *m*

**control** [kən'trəʊl] *vt* (*master*) beherrschen; (*temper etc*) im Griff haben; (*esp Tech*) steuern; **to ~ oneself** sich beherrschen ▷ *n* Kontrolle *f*; (*mastery*) Beherrschung *f*; (*of business*) Leitung *f*; (*esp Tech*) Steuerung *f*; **~s** *pl* (*knobs, switches etc*) Bedienungselemente *pl*; (*collectively*) Steuerung *f*; **to be out of ~** außer Kontrolle sein; **control knob** *n* Bedienungsknopf *m*; **control panel** *n* Schalttafel *f*

**controversial** [kɒntrə'vɜːʃəl] *adj* umstritten

**convalesce** [kɒnvə'lɛs] *vi* gesund werden; **convalescence** *n* Genesung *f*

**convenience** [kən'viːnɪəns] *n* (*quality, thing*) Annehmlichkeit *f*; **at your ~** wann es Ihnen passt; **with all modern ~s** mit allem Komfort; **convenience food** *n* Fertiggericht *nt*; **convenient** *adj* günstig, passend

**convent** ['kɒnvənt] *n* Kloster *nt*

**convention** [kən'vɛnʃən] *n* (*custom*) Konvention *f*; (*meeting*) Konferenz *f*; **the Geneva Convention** die Genfer Konvention; **conventional** *adj* herkömmlich, konventionell

**conversation** [kɒnvə'seɪʃən] *n* Gespräch *nt*, Unterhaltung *f*

**conversion** [kən'vɜːʃən] *n* Umwandlung *f* (*into* in +*akk*); (*of building*) Umbau *m* (*into* zu); (*calculation*) Umrechnung *f*;

**conversion table** *n* Umrechnungstabelle *f*; **convert** [kən'vɜːt] *vt* umwandeln; (*person*) bekehren; (*Inform*) konvertieren; **to ~ into Euros** in Euro umrechnen; **convertible** *n* (*Auto*) Kabrio *nt* ▷ *adj* umwandelbar

**convey** [kən'veɪ] *vt* (*carry*) befördern; (*feelings*) vermitteln; **conveyor belt** *n* Förderband *nt*, Fließband *nt*

**convict** [kən'vɪkt] *vt* verurteilen (*of* wegen*) ▷ ['kɒnvɪkt] *n* Strafgefangene(r) *mf*; **conviction** *n* (*Jur*) Verurteilung *f*; (*strong belief*) Überzeugung *f*

**convince** [kən'vɪns] *vt* überzeugen (*of* von); **convincing** *adj* überzeugend

**cook** [kʊk] *vt, vi* kochen ▷ *n* Koch *m*, Köchin *f*; **cookbook** *n* Kochbuch *nt*; **cooker** *n* Herd *m*; **cookery** *n* Kochkunst *f*; **~ book** Kochbuch *nt*; **cookie** *n* (*US*) Keks *m*; **cooking** *n* Kochen *nt*; (*style of cooking*) Küche *f*

**cool** [kuːl] *adj* kühl, gelassen; (*fam: brilliant*) cool, stark ▷ *vt, vi* (ab)kühlen; **~ it** reg dich ab! ▷ *n* **to keep/lose one's ~** (*fam*) ruhig bleiben/durchdrehen; **cool down** *vi* abkühlen; (*calm down*) sich beruhigen

**cooperate** [kəʊ'ɒpəreɪt] *vi* zusammenarbeiten, kooperieren; **cooperation** [kəʊɒpə'reɪʃən] *n* Zusammenarbeit *f*, Kooperation *f*; **cooperative** [kəʊ'ɒpərətɪv] *adj* hilfsbereit ▷ *n* Genossenschaft *f*

**coordinate** [kəʊ'ɔːdɪneɪt] *vt* koordinieren

**cop** [kɒp] *n* (*fam: policeman*) Bulle *m*

**cope** [kəʊp] *vi* zurechtkommen, fertig werden (*with* mit)

**Copenhagen** [kəʊpən'heɪgən] *n* Kopenhagen *nt*

**copier** ['kɒpɪə*] *n* Kopierer *m*

**copper** ['kɒpə*] *n* Kupfer *nt*; (*Brit fam: policeman*) Bulle *m*; (*fam: coin*) Kupfermünze *f*; **~s** Kleingeld *nt*

**copy** ['kɒpɪ] *n* Kopie *f*; (*of book*) Exemplar *nt* ▷ *vt* kopieren; (*imitate*) nachahmen; **copyright** *n* Urheberrecht *nt*

**coral** ['kɒrəl] *n* Koralle *f*

**cord** [kɔːd] *n* Schnur *f*; (*material*) Kordsamt *m*

**cordial** ['kɔːdɪəl] *adj* freundlich

**cordless** ['kɔːdlɪs] *adj* (*phone*) schnurlos

**core** [kɔː*] *n* (*a. fig*) Kern *m*; (*of apple, pear*)